# BRAAI

Struik Publishers (a division of
New Holland Publishing
(South Africa) (Pty) Ltd)
Cornelis Struik House
80 McKenzie Street
Cape Town 8001

New Holland Publishing is
a member of Avusa Ltd.
Visit us at **www.struik.co.za**

First published in 2008

1  2  3  4  5  6  7  8  9  10

**Publishing manager:** Linda de Villiers
**Managing editor:** Cecilia Barfield
**Editors:** Irma van Wyk, Gill Gordon
**Designer:** Helen Henn

Reproduction by Hirt & Carter Cape (Pty) Ltd
Printed and bound by Craft Print International
Pte Ltd, Singapore

ISBN 978 177007 506 1

Log on to our photographic website
www.imagesofafrica.co.za for an
African experience.

# Contents

# Introduction

Cooking over a flame is intertwined with South African culture. Not many people can resist the unmistakeable aroma of food cooked on a braai. It's our favourite way of eating and entertaining. Braaiing has evolved from a rudimentary wood fire for 'chops and wors' into a whole culture of state-of-the-art equipment, recipe books, gadgets and gizmos.

## DIFFERENT TYPES OF BRAAI

### GAS BRAAIS

The most basic gas braai consists of a gas bottle with a grid, *skottel* (dish or basin), solid griddle or potjie attachment. Gas braais are portable and can be used anywhere. They are not very large and are not suitable for cooking on a large scale, unless more than one is available.

### Weber Q Gas Braai

These come in a variety of sizes, Weber Q 100, 200 and 300. They can be used for direct as well as indirect methods (page 10) of cooking. For indirect cooking, the cast-iron grid gets very hot, so you need to turn the flame down and place the items for cooking in the middle of the grid. A variety of attachments are available.

### Large, free-standing

These are available in a variety of sizes with an assortment of attachments as well as a rotisserie. Larger free-standing braais have the option of a griddle section as well as a solid plate section. Most also have a single gas ring on the side, which can hold a pot. The gas can be varied for indirect cooking. Generally, these braais are not portable because of their size.

### Built-in

Built-in gas braais are very popular, especially in indoor braai rooms. Always ensure that there is a safe, well-ventilated place for the gas bottle to be stored.

### CHARCOAL BRAAIS

Charcoal braais can be as basic as a hole in the ground and as sophisticated as a kettle braai.

### Half-drum

This is half a 44-gallon drum that has been mounted onto legs. Because of its size, it is not very portable; however, if on wheels, it can easily be moved. A half-drum braai should always have holes in the base for air circulation and to help dispose of burned ashes. Usually clay bricks are put in the base and the fire built on top of them. Normally this kind of braai does not have much more than a grid to cook on and the cooking height cannot be adjusted very easily. However, because of their size, they are very useful for cooking large quantities of meat.

### Portable

These are available in many sizes and come with a range of attachments. There are portable braais to suit all your requirements.

### The 'Cob'

This is a very useful portable braai that works on the same principle as a kettle braai. It is best for cooking small portions, such as a whole chicken or other roasts.

### Built-in

These are very fashionable and one can hardly find a townhouse or home that doesn't have one already built in. Built-in braais vary from the very basic to the ultra sophisticated, which include adjustable shelves and a rotisserie.

## THE KETTLE BRAAI

The kettle grill was invented in 1951 by an American called George Stephen, who was an avid braai buff but found that the flat grill didn't work well in rainy and windy weather. At the time, he was working for Weber Brothers Metal Works, a manufacturer of nautical buoys. He had the idea of fitting a metal grate into one of the spun metal bowls used for buoy making. He then made a cover with vents from the same metal. In 1952 he marketed his grill as 'George's Kettle'.

The advantage of the deep-covered kettle grill was that, as well as deflecting wind and rain, it transformed an ordinary grill into an oven that could roast food. Today the Weber® Kettle grill remains the world's best-selling charcoal grill.

## ELECTRIC TABLETOP GRILLS

Tabletop grills are fuelled by electricity. They are preheated; some have a variable heat control while others have just one setting. When piping hot, they can be used to cook any meat or vegetable that uses the direct heat method of cooking. Their disadvantage is that they can only be used where there is a supply of electricity.

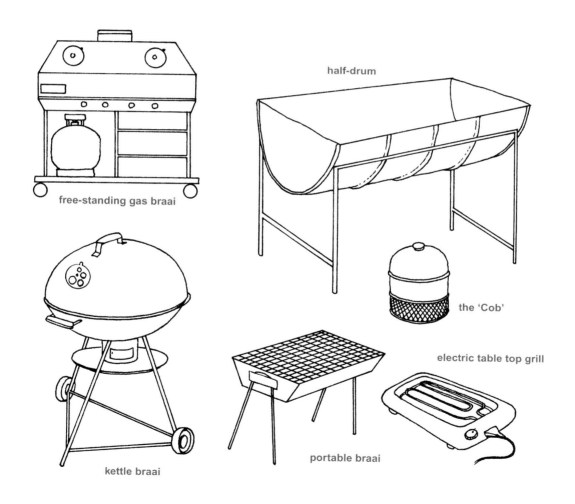

free-standing gas braai

half-drum

the 'Cob'

kettle braai

portable braai

electric table top grill

*Braais come in many shapes and sizes, so you are sure to find one that suits your needs.*

# TIPS FOR BUYING A BRAAI

- **BUDGET:** Decide what you can afford to spend on a braai, then look at the available products in your price range.
- **NEEDS:** Buy the product that will suit your needs. Decide on the size and whether you would prefer charcoal or gas – weigh up the advantages and disadvantages of each.
- **CONSTRUCTION:** Whatever type of braai you choose, make sure it is sturdily constructed; if it appears rickety on the shop floor, it will most likely fall apart in your back yard.
- **QUALITY OF THE GRATES:** Good-quality grills have grates that are made of cast iron, stainless steel or porcelain-covered aluminium.

# BRAAI ACCESSORIES

There are a few essential accessories that the serious braaier must have, and then there are those 'nice-to-have' accessories that you just cannot resist when browsing the shelves of speciality stores. These also make great gifts for the braai enthusiast.

## ESSENTIAL EQUIPMENT
- **TONGS:** Preferably long-handled, to avoid getting your fingers scorched.
- **LONG-PRONGED FORK:** Use this only for lifting large roasts and poultry from the grill. Never poke meat with a fork during cooking, as this will result in the loss of all the natural juices.
- **BASTING BRUSH:** A brush is essential for basting meat with marinade during cooking. If possible, choose one with a long handle. If using a short-handled brush, it is advisable to use an oven glove, as the addition of marinades can sometimes cause flare-ups. The brush should preferably have natural bristles; many modern ones are made from silicone. Plastic bristles are not suitable, as they are likely to melt.

- **APRON:** Some people may object to wearing an apron, but you can save yourself a lot of food splashes if you cover up while braaiing.
- **SPRAY BOTTLE:** A cheap, plastic spray bottle purchased from a hardware store and filled with water is essential to have on hand; it is useful when flare-ups occur.
- **LONG MATCHES** OR A **LONG-NOSE GAS LIGHTER:** These are essential for lighting charcoal braais.
- **DRIP TRAYS:** If you have one of these positioned beneath the grill to catch dripping juices and marinades, it will make cleaning up afterwards so much easier. Drip trays are used for indirect cooking. Buy one according to the size of your braai. Foil containers can be used several times before being discarded.
- **WIRE BRUSH AND SCRAPER:** Essential for cleaning the grill after the braai.

## NICE-TO-HAVE ACCESSORIES
- **MEAT THERMOMETER:** This is used for large cuts of meat. There are very cheap, basic thermometers available with a probe that pierces the thickest part of the meat and shows a reading on a dial. You can also purchase battery-operated digital thermometers that provide an instant reading when inserted into meat. Thermometers do take the guesswork out of judging whether thick meat cuts are cooked to the right degree of doneness.
- **WIDE SPATULA:** In metal or teflon, this is useful for turning vegetables and essential when cooking eggs on a flat griddle.
- **FISH HOLDER:** This is a stainless steel, hinged basket shaped like a fish and normally holds a medium to large fish. It makes handling and turning a whole fish much easier.
- **VEGETABLE TRAY:** This stainless steel tray has holes in the base and is used in a kettle braai. Vegetables are placed in the tray, then onto the braai.

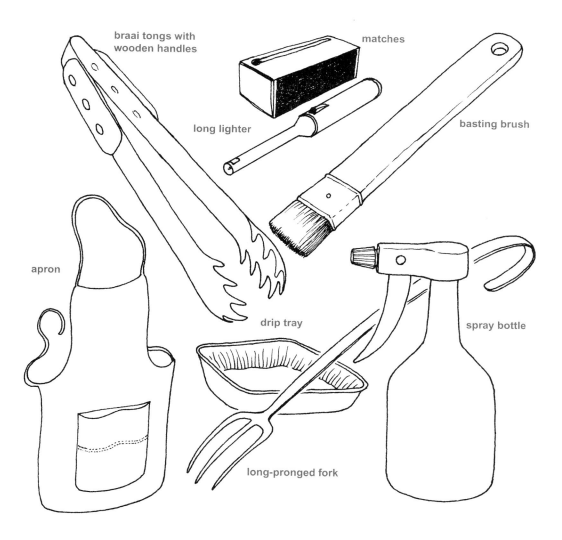

braai tongs with wooden handles

matches

long lighter

basting brush

apron

drip tray

spray bottle

long-pronged fork

*Braai accessories range from the 'must-'have' to the 'nice-to-have'; these are some of the essentials.*

- **RIB RACK:** A specially designed item for holding racks of ribs; makes handling and cooking much easier.
- **BRAAI BIRD:** The braai bird is a gimmicky attachment that holds a can of beer onto which a whole chicken is mounted and roasted using the indirect cooking method.
- **WOK, PAELLA AND PIZZA PANS:** These are used for making specific dishes and are very practical when feeding a large crowd.
- **CHIMNEY STARTER:** This is a container in which extra coals are readied for a charcoal braai. When items such as large roasts or turkeys are cooked, the fire needs to be replenished regularly and the extra coals made in the chimney starter can be added to the fire when they are needed. (See also page 10: Adding extra coals.)
- **GRILL COVERS:** Canvas or PVC covers are available in different shapes and sizes, and will help keep dust and dirt off your braai, especially if it is stored outside.

# LIGHTING THE FIRE

## WOOD

Although wood was the original fuel used to make a braai, many braai lovers have switched to the convenience of charcoal and gas. But, for the purist, nothing beats the distinctive flavour that wood adds to braaied meat. Bags of pre-cut wood can be conveniently purchased from petrol stations, supermarkets, convenience stores and along the roadside in many towns.

Look out for a hard wood that will produce long-lasting coals for the braai. Some suitable South African woods are camel thorn, rooikrans, vine sticks (particularly in the Western Cape), mopane, leadwood and bush-willow. Certain woods, such as tamboti and oleander, which give off a poisonous gas when burnt, should not be used. Take care not to use treated wood (wood that has been painted or varnished).

A wood braai requires large amounts of wood, kindling and paper. Today there are far more efficient and environmentally friendly fuels available.

## CHARCOAL

Charcoal is made from hardwood or lump wood and is available as lump wood charcoal and charcoal briquettes. Charcoal briquettes are uniformly shaped lumps of fuel and burn for longer than lump wood charcoal. Charcoal lights easily – even better with firelighters – and burns for a good length of time. Choose a quality charcoal briquette. On the local market, there are a number of brands to choose from.

For longer burning fires, indirect cooking requires twice the amount of charcoal than needed for direct cooking; one layer of charcoal arranged slightly wider than the food to be cooked will be sufficient.

It takes approximately 30 minutes for charcoal briquettes to burn down to coals. When the briquettes are covered with a layer of light grey ash they should be ready for braaiing. It is important to ensure that charcoal does not get wet or it won't ignite.

## GAS

Gas braais are extremely convenient and are a popular choice. Gas is a spontaneous fuel that is easily controlled for cooking outdoors. Gas comes in cylinders that need to be filled at specialist suppliers. Highly flammable, gas cylinders should be stored upright and away from direct heat, and must be fitted with a regulator for safe operation. Do not smoke while working with a gas flame. Ensure that the gas is switched off when the cooking is completed.

# SETTING UP THE BRAAI

Being prepared is the key to a successful braai, so it is essential to ensure that the fire is made with a good-quality dry charcoal or briquettes and lit well in advance of cooking time. Heat control is the next most important aspect. Before any meat is placed on the braai, the coals should be glowing red and coated with a film of white-grey ash.

## BUILDING THE FIRE

The amount of charcoal you use depends on how much and what kind of food you intend to braai. The more food you will be cooking, the longer the fire needs to burn hot. Bear in mind that it is easier to reduce the heat than to raise it so, as a general rule, start out with more charcoal than you think you may need.

There is an art to lighting a fire. An average gas braai will be ready for cooking in 10 to 15 minutes after lighting, but charcoal needs more time, and will be ready only 30 to 40 minutes after lighting. The simplest way to start a fire is to heap charcoal in the centre of the braai and to add one or two pieces of broken up firelighters. Light the firelighters and allow the charcoal to burn down to hot coals. Do not use more charcoal or briquettes in the belief that the fire will burn for longer; it will just be much hotter, but will burn out just as quickly.

After practising several times, you will be able to gauge just how much fuel is needed but, as a guide, a couple of layers of charcoal or a packed single layer of charcoal briquettes will provide sufficient heat to keep a braai fire going for 1–1$\frac{1}{2}$ hours.

## GETTING THE HEAT JUST RIGHT

- **HOT:** This is when the flames have died down and the coals are glowing red and covered with a layer of white-grey ash. You should be able to hold your hand 15 cm above the coals for 2 seconds. This is the temperature at which 'thin' foods such as fish fillets, flattened pieces of chicken and meat can be cooked, but anything thicker will burn on the outside and still be raw on the inside. However, this is be the correct temperature for cooking rare steaks.
- **MEDIUM:** As the ash gets thicker and the heat decreases, this is the temperature that suits most foods. You should be able to hold your hand over the fire for 4 seconds.
- **COOL:** When the ash is very thick and powdery, the coals crumble and collapse when touched, and there is no red glow peeping through, the heat is low. If you can hold your hand over the coals for 6 seconds or more, the heat is too cool for cooking. At this point extra coals may be added, as they will ignite. After 15 to 20 minutes, the fire temperature will be ready for cooking again.

## CHANGING THE TEMPERATURE

The heat can be altered a little during cooking. To increase the temperature, move the coals around to knock off the ash, then pile them up again in the centre of the braai.

If the fire is too hot, carefully spread out the coals and close any air vents in the base for a few minutes. If your braai has a lid, use it with the air vents closed to reduce the temperature quickly. Spraying a little water over the coals will also help reduce the heat, but be careful of the steam that is emitted.

Stacking the coals high on one side and low on the other is also a way of controlling the cooking. Start the meat on high to seal it, then move it to low to cook more slowly.

Another way of regulating the heat once the coals have built up a coating of ash is to move the grill rack up and down. However, this will not be effective if the coals are still red hot, as any unprotected food (food that is not wrapped in foil) will quickly burn black regardless of the

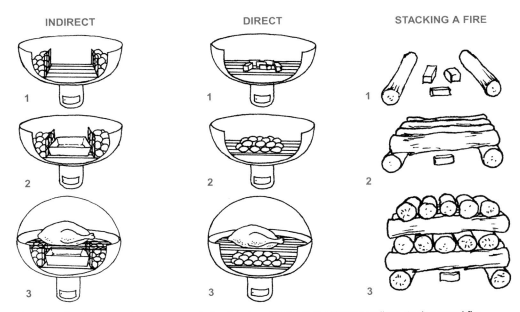

| INDIRECT | DIRECT | STACKING A FIRE |

*These diagrams illustrate how to prepare coals for direct and indirect cooking as well as stack a wood fire.*

height above the coals. If time is short, move the coals aside using tongs, put a drip tray in place and cook with a lid over indirect heat.

## ADDING EXTRA COALS

An easy and safe way to add extra coals to a fire is to use a chimney starter (see page 7). This is a metal, tube-shaped device that has air holes in the sides. Place crumpled newspaper or firelighters in the base and fill the space above the paper with coals. Ignite the newspaper and eventually the coals will burn. Once the coals are dusted with ash, tip them into the braai and spread them out evenly.

# DIRECT AND INDIRECT COOKING

If you have ever braaied food that was charred on the outside and not quite cooked on the inside, the chances are that you were using the wrong cooking method or that the fire was too hot. Direct and indirect cooking methods are the main ones used when braaiing, and achieving success with both is as simple as setting up for the right method.

## DIRECT COOKING

Direct cooking is the traditional method of braaiing – in which food is placed on the grill and cooked directly over the coals. As a general rule, foods that take less than 25 minutes to cook are cooked by the direct cooking method and can be done on various types of braai, either with or without a lid.

Direct cooking needs constant attention, as the food is positioned directly over the heat source and can burn if left unattended.

Start the fire and then leave the coals to burn for 40–45 minutes before starting to cook. For a medium-hot braai, you'll need approximately 60 briquettes; but for a lower temperature, around 45 briquettes should be sufficient. Spread the prepared coals evenly over the charcoal grate. Set the cooking grate above the coals and place the food directly onto it.

## INDIRECT COOKING

Foods that require longer cooking times are cooked by the indirect method, which is done in a covered braai. In the case of gas, the burners directly beneath the food are turned off while the side burners remain on. In the case of charcoal, metal bars that hold two stacks of coals are placed against the sides of the braai, leaving the centre clear. A disposable foil dish is placed in the empty space to collect fat drips.

Leave the fire to develop for about 45 minutes. Place the cooking grid over the fire and place the food in such a way that it is positioned over the drip tray, then cover with the lid. Keep the bottom vents open so that the heat circulates more evenly. Don't open the lid more than you have to – the more often the heat is allowed to escape, the longer the cooking time will be.

Extra coals can be made in a chimney starter (see page 7), an old metal bucket or even on the ground in a sandy area and added to the fire so as not to lower the temperature too drastically.

## SMOKING

When smoking meat, wood chips are used and the flavour of the food is affected by the choice of wood used. A variety of wood chips are available for smoking, but hickory and oak are the best known.

Wood chips have to be pre-soaked in cold water for about 1 hour so that they will smoulder slowly over the fire, rather than burn. Once soaked, add 1–2 cups of soaked, drained wood chips to the coals when you start to braai and again when the coals are replenished. For additional flavour, soak a variety of herbs in the water along with the wood chips, then sprinkle the herbs over the coals. Smoking is best suited to moderate to slow cooking.

## CLEANING

Take time to empty and clean out the braai after every use. Use a sturdy wire brush to remove grime from the grill rack. Wash the rack regularly otherwise the food cooked on it could taste of stale, burnt grease.

# HOW LONG DOES FOOD TAKE TO COOK?

It is vital to make sure that meat, particularly poultry, is properly cooked through. Appearances may be deceptive – food can be charred on the outside, but raw on the inside. It's best to turn food only once during cooking and not repeatedly, which can make it tough.

However, if the meat has been marinated and only if the marinade has a high sugar content, it may be necessary to turn it frequently to prevent burning.

Cooking times are a general guide – factors that can influence cooking times include the temperature outside, the heat of the coals and the wind factor.

## FACTORS INFLUENCING COOKING TIMES OF MEAT

Apart from ensuring the correct cooking method, everybody has a preference for how they like their meat cooked. The cut and thickness of the meat, how hot the braai is and the distance of the food from the heat source are all factors that are important in determining how the meat will eventually turn out.

Meat from a young animal is more tender and needs a shorter cooking time than meat from an older animal. Mature, ripened beef cooks more quickly than freshly slaughtered meat.

As the temperature of meat before cooking will also determine the cooking time, meat should always be brought to room temperature before cooking. The thickness of the cut also has an effect on the cooking time.

## THE PERFECT STEAK

These timings are approximate for a 3-cm thick steak cooked over medium-high heat. For large cuts of meat, determine the degree of doneness by inserting a traditional thermometer into the thickest part of the meat, ensuring that it does not touch the bone.

- **RARE 65 °C:** Cook for 2 minutes on each side. The steak should feel quite soft when lightly pressed and the inside will be very red and juicy throughout.
- **MEDIUM-RARE 65–70 °C:** Cook each side for about 3 minutes. The steak will feel quite soft when lightly pressed, but the inside will be less red with pink juices.
- **MEDIUM 70 °C:** Cook the steak for 4 minutes on each side. The meat will feel slightly springy to the touch and should still be pink in the middle but browned around the edges. The juices should run pale pink.
- **WELL DONE 75 °C:** Sear the steak until the meat juices start collecting on top then turn and cook until the juices have collected again. At this stage, reduce the heat slightly so that the steak can continue to cook through without burning. It should be cooked for about 5 minutes on each side. The steak should be quite firm when pressed, and will not be pink inside. A well-done steak does tend to be rather dry, no matter what cut of meat is used.

## TOUCH TEST FOR MEAT

The texture of meat becomes firmer as heat penetrates from the surface towards the centre. Gently press the thickest part of the meat with your fingertip. The softer the meat, the more rare it is; the firmer the feel, the more well done it is.

## TEST FOR FISH

Use a fork to test fish. Fish is cooked when the flesh is firm and it is just beginning to flake; it should be opaque through the centre but still moist.

## TEST FOR CHICKEN

Using a small, sharp knife, make a small, deep cut into the thickest part of chicken. The flesh should be cooked throughout with no trace of pink at the bone.

# COOKING TIMES

| Fish and shellfish | |
|---|---|
| Don't try to cook flaky fish, such as hake, on the braai, as it will fall apart; rather stick to firmer fish. Also, don't overcook seafood. | |
| Fish fillets or steaks, 2 cm thick | 5–10 minutes |
| Fish kebabs, bite-sized chunks on skewers | 8–10 minutes |
| Whole fish, less than 1 kg | 15–20 minutes |
| Large whole fish, 1–2 kg | 30–45 minutes kettle braai only; indirect heat |
| Prawns (medium–large), raw in their shells on skewers | 4–6 minutes |
| Crayfish (500–650 g), split open lengthways | 10–15 minutes |

| Vegetables | |
|---|---|
| Most vegetables can be cooked on the braai with great results. | |
| Asparagus, whole spears | 5–6 minutes |
| Baby marrows, halved lengthways | 8–15 minutes |
| Brinjals, cut 1 cm thick | 8–10 minutes |
| Mealies | 15–20 minutes |
| Fennel bulbs, cut into 4 thick slices | 10–12 minutes |
| Large mushrooms, whole, on double skewers | 8–10 minutes |
| Peppers, halves or quarters | 6–8 minutes |
| Red onions, wedges on skewers | 10–12 minutes |
| Sweet potatoes (sliced and covered in foil) | 45 minutes |
| Tomato halves, cut-side up | 6–8 minutes |
| Jacket potatoes cooked in foil | 40–50 minutes |

| Sausages | |
|---|---|
| Thick | 15–18 minutes |

| Burgers | |
|---|---|
| 2 cm thick | 10 minutes |

| Kebabs | |
|---|---|
| Bite-sized chunks on skewers | 10–12 minutes |

| Beef | |
|---|---|
| Whole fillet (1.5 kg) | 25–30 minutes; indirect heat only |
| Steaks | (2.5 cm thick) |
|   Rare | 6 minutes |
|   Medium | 8 minutes |
|   Well done | 10 minutes |

| Lamb | |
|---|---|
| Chops and cutlets | 10–12 minutes |
| Fillet, boneless | 10–12 minutes |
| Leg, butterflied (1–1.5 kg) medium done | 35–45 minutes |
| Leg roast, boned and rolled (1.3-1.6 kg) | $1\frac{1}{2}$–$1\frac{3}{4}$ hours, kettle braai only; indirect heat |

| Pork | |
|---|---|
| Ribs | 10–20 minutes, turning often |
| Steaks, boneless | 10 minutes |
| Chops, bone-in | 10 minutes |
| Fillet whole roast | 20–30 minutes |

| Chicken, turkey and duck | |
|---|---|
| Chicken breasts, boneless | 10 minutes |
| Chicken thighs, boneless | 8–10 minutes |
| Chicken breasts, on the bone | 30–35 minutes |
| Chicken thighs/drumsticks, on the bone | 35–40 minutes |
| Chicken, whole roast (1.3–1.6 kg) | $1$–$1\frac{1}{2}$ hours, kettle braai only; indirect heat |
| Turkey, steaks | 6–8 minutes |
| Turkey, whole roast | 3–4 hours |
| Duck, whole roast (1.8–2 kg) | $1\frac{1}{2}$–$2$ hours, kettle braai only; indirect heat |
| Duck breasts | 5 minutes on each side; indirect heat |

# TOP TIPS FOR A GOOD BRAAI

- Never use petrol to try to start a braai.
- Never leave a braai unattended.
- Remember that even if you are using a gas braai, it needs to be preheated for approximately 10–15 minutes before using. Charcoal or wood fires can take up to an hour to attain the correct heat.
- Always use tongs to turn food on the braai. Forks or sharp objects pierce the food, causing a loss of flavourful juices.
- Braai meat in the correct order – boerewors, sausages, chops. Braai steaks last to prevent them from becoming tough.
- Meat and chicken should be seasoned with salt just before cooking, as salt draws out the meat juices and makes it tough.
- It's always a good idea to keep a spray bottle filled with water handy to douse flame flare-ups. Beer works well too.
- Ensure that the braai is really hot, but not too hot, before you begin cooking. The coals should be glowing red and covered with a layer of pale grey ash.
- Never rush when cooking on the braai. Make sure that all the food, particularly chicken, is cooked through. Don't assume that food that is charred on the outside will be cooked on the inside. To test if meat is cooked, pierce the thickest part of the meat and, if the juices run clear, the food is cooked.
- Toss small branches of the bay tree or rosemary bush over a charcoal or wood fire before cooking – this gives the food a lovely aroma. The branches don't need to be soaked beforehand.
- Keep raw and cooked or partially cooked meat separately, as the raw meat juices may come into contact with the cooked meat.
- Remember that most marinades contain sugar or other sweet ingredients that burn very quickly over the flames. Remove as much marinade as possible from meat/chicken before placing over the grill. Marinade can be served as an accompaniment but must be cooked separately before serving because it contains raw meat juices.
- If combining meat or chicken on a skewer with vegetables, ensure that everything is cut into equally sized portions in order to cook evenly.
- Clean braais thoroughly after use.

*A brush is essential for basting meat with marinade during cooking.*

# Meat

# Beef

## Sweet Chilli Beef Skewers
Serves 4

500 g rump steak
45 ml sweet chilli sauce
60 ml plum sauce
45 ml soy sauce
10 ml sesame oil
15 ml fish sauce

2 cloves garlic, chopped
15 ml chopped fresh or 5 ml ground ginger
30 ml chopped fresh coriander
45 ml peanut oil
1 red onion, cut into wedges
wooden skewers, soaked in water for 30 minutes

1  Cut the meat into 2 cm cubes.
2  Combine all the remaining ingredients except the onions, then add the meat.
3  Marinate for at least 4 hours or overnight.
4  Thread the meat alternately with the onion wedges onto the skewers. Cook over a high heat for about 10 minutes, turning once or twice, until the meat is medium rare.

## Steak with Fresh Herb Marinade
Serves 4

160 ml olive oil
30 ml chopped fresh thyme
30 ml chopped fresh parsley
15 ml chopped fresh rosemary
1 red chilli, seeded and chopped
15 ml paprika

3 cloves garlic, chopped
45 ml red wine vinegar
salt and freshly ground black pepper to taste
800 g steak (aged rump, sirloin or rib-eye
  is suitable)

1  Heat the olive oil until just hot, remove from the heat and add all the remaining ingredients except the steak. Leave to infuse for about 1 hour.
2  Place half the marinade into a non-metallic dish and add the steak. Marinate in the fridge for 1–2 hours. Reserve the remaining marinade to serve with the steak.
3  Remove the meat from the fridge and bring to room temperature. Cook over hot coals for about 2–4 minutes per side until medium-rare, depending on the thickness of the meat.
4  Rest for 5 minutes before cutting the steak into slices across the grain. Bring the reserved marinade to the boil in a small saucepan and serve with the steak.

*Steak with Fresh Herb Marinade, Strawberry and Asparagus Salad*
*with Parmesan Crisps (page 137) and Olive Oil Bread (page 126)*

*Fillet in Beer Sauce*

# Fillet in Beer Sauce
Serves 6

80 ml ready-made barbecue sauce

30 ml whole grain mustard

3 cloves garlic, chopped

60 ml olive oil

250 ml beer

800 g–1 kg beef fillet

1  Combine all the ingredients except the beef, and mix well. Marinate the whole fillet in the sauce overnight.
2  Place the meat in a disposable foil container and cook, using the indirect heat in a kettle braai (see page 10), for 40–50 minutes until desired doneness. Baste frequently with the sauce.
3  Rest for 5 minutes before slicing thinly.


# Sesame and Ginger Beef Fillet
Serves 6

45 ml sesame oil

60 ml soy sauce

3 cloves garlic, crushed

45 ml chopped fresh ginger

30 ml lemon juice

1 bunch spring onions, finely chopped

80 ml soft brown sugar

800 g–1 kg beef fillet

1  Combine all the ingredients, add the beef and marinate overnight.
2  Brown the meat on all sides over a high heat. Remove from the heat, wrap in foil and seal well. Return to the heat and cook using indirect heat (see page 10) for 30–40 minutes, turning occasionally, until cooked to desired doneness.
3  Place the marinade into a small saucepan, bring to the boil and simmer for 5 minutes. When the meat is done, rest for 5 minutes before slicing and serving with the marinade.


# Beef, Mushroom and Bacon Kebabs
Serves 4

100 ml red wine

45 ml olive oil

2 cloves garlic, chopped

1 bunch spring onions, finely chopped

30 ml tomato paste

sprig fresh thyme

salt and freshly ground black pepper

500 g rib-eye steaks, cut into 2 cm cubes

250 g smoked streaky bacon

250 g button mushrooms

oil

4 wooden skewers, soaked in water for 30 minutes

1  Combine the red wine, olive oil, garlic, spring onions, tomato paste, thyme and seasoning, and mix well. Add the meat cubes and marinate for at least 4 hours or overnight.
2  Roll up the rashers of bacon into tight rolls and thread onto the soaked skewers, alternating with the cubes of beef and the mushrooms. Brush the mushrooms with a little oil.
3  Grill over medium-hot coals for 8–10 minutes until the meat is medium rare and the bacon is cooked.

# Steak in Cola Marinade

*The cola has a tenderising effect on the meat*

Serves 4

15 ml olive oil

1 onion, chopped

2 cloves garlic, chopped

15 ml chopped fresh ginger

1 red chilli, seeded and chopped

1 x 340 ml can cola

180 ml tomato sauce

grated rind of 1 lemon

30 ml lemon juice

15 ml whole grain mustard

30 ml white wine vinegar

800 g steak (aged rump, rib-eye or sirloin)

1  Heat the oil and gently fry the onion, garlic, ginger and chilli until softened. Add the remaining ingredients except the steak and simmer for 20 minutes, then cool.

2  Pour about 250 ml over the steak and reserve the remainder for serving. Marinate the meat, covered, in the fridge overnight. Drain off the marinade.

3  Bring the meat to room temperature before cooking over medium-high heat until desired doneness. Rest for 5 minutes before slicing across the grain. Serve with the reserved sauce, which has been heated through thoroughly.


# Blackened Beef with Saffron Mayonnaise

Serves 4

2 cloves garlic, crushed

15 ml chopped fresh ginger

3 chillies, seeded and sliced

10 ml fennel seeds

3 ml turmeric

5 ml ground coriander

1 small onion, finely chopped

1 small beef fillet or whole sirloin

**SAFFRON MAYONNAISE**

250 ml olive oil

1 egg yolk

10 ml lime or lemon juice

1 generous pinch saffron threads

10 ml hot water

coarse sea salt

1  Make a paste with the garlic, ginger and chillies in a mortar and pestle. Add the fennel seeds and turmeric. Blend in the coriander and onion. Rub the paste onto the fillet or sirloin. Massage it into the meat, cover and set aside at room temperature for 1 hour.

2  While the meat is marinating, make the mayonnaise by whisking the olive oil into the egg yolk drop by drop using a food processor. Add the lime or lemon juice and keep whisking until the mixture thickens. Add the saffron threads to the hot water, then blend this into the mayonnaise and season with the coarse salt.

3  Roast the beef over high heat on a griddle or over a braai until medium-rare or cooked as desired. Slice and serve with the saffron mayonnaise and a salad.

*Blackened Beef with Saffron Mayonnaise and Roasted Butternut and Chickpea Salad (page 141)*

*Boerewors Bites, Vegetarian Skewers (page 105) and Beef, Mushroom and Bacon Kebabs (page 21)*

# Boerewors Bites
Makes 8–10

1 kg boerewors
200 g cheddar or mozzarella cheese, sliced
250 g rindless streaky bacon

a large handful fresh basil
1 punnet cocktail tomatoes
toothpicks

1  Cut the boerewors into 6 cm pieces and cut open lengthwise without cutting right through. Insert a slice of cheese and close by wrapping a piece of bacon around the boerewors. Secure with a toothpick.
2  Cook over the coals until golden brown on both sides. Garnish with a fresh basil leaf and cocktail tomato secured onto a toothpick. Serve warm.

# Basic Beef Burgers
Makes 8

100 g bread (± 2 slices)
water for soaking the bread
500 g lean minced beef
1 onion, finely chopped
30 ml soy sauce

10 ml whole grain mustard
freshly ground black pepper to taste
5 ml chopped fresh thyme
15 ml chopped fresh parsley

1  Remove the crusts from the bread and soak in a little water until pulpy.
2  Combine all the ingredients in the bowl of a food processor and process for a few minutes until combined.
3  Wet the hands and shape into 8 patties. Rest the burgers in the fridge before cooking.
4  Cook on a lightly oiled braai grid for about 5 minutes on each side until lightly browned and cooked through.
5  Serve on bread rolls with slices of tomato, onion and your choice of sauce.

# Sweet and Sour Kebabs

Serves 4

15 ml oil

2 onions, sliced

5 ml turmeric

2 ml ground coriander

5 ml curry powder

5 ml finely chopped fresh ginger

2 bay leaves

120 g brown sugar

25 ml chutney

5 ml salt

25 ml flour

250 ml water

25 ml vinegar

500 g rump steak, cubed

250 g pork fillet, cubed

8 wooden skewers, soaked in water for 30 minutes

1   Heat the oil and lightly fry the onions in a medium-sized saucepan. Add the spices and herbs, and fry for 1 minute. Add the sugar, chutney and salt. Stir in the flour, then add the water and vinegar.
2   Bring to the boil, reduce the heat and simmer, covered, for 15 minutes, then cool.
3   Thread the meat onto the wooden skewers. Lay the sticks in a shallow glass dish, pour over the cooled sauce and leave overnight. Drain off the excess marinade and set aside.
4   Cook the kebabs over medium coals on the braai, basting occasionally with the reserved marinade for 10–15 minutes or until the meat is cooked. Bring the remaining sauce to a boil and serve over the kebabs.


# Espetada

Serves 4–6

1 kg rump steak, about 25 mm thick

60 ml olive oil

60 ml red wine vinegar

1 onion, finely chopped

125 ml chopped parsley

20 ml crushed garlic

5 ml salt

5 ml freshly ground black pepper

12 bay leaves

4–6 wooden skewers, soaked in water
      for 30 minutes

coarse salt

1   Trim the excess fat and sinew off the meat and cut into 3 cm cubes.
2   Combine the remaining ingredients, except the salt, in a large bowl. Add the beef and toss to coat. Cover and leave to marinate overnight.
3   Thread the meat onto the skewers, sprinkle lightly with the coarse salt and cook over medium coals on the braai for 5 minutes on each side or until the meat is done to your liking. Baste with any excess marinade during cooking.

*Sweet and Sour Kebabs, Beef and Onion Kebabs (page 29) and Cheese and Onion Quick Bread (page 127)*

*Surprise Beef Parcels*

# Beef and Onion Kebabs

Serves 4

800 g rump steak
20 pickling (baby) onions, peeled
8 wooden skewers, soaked in water for 30 minutes

MARINADE
100 ml tomato sauce
45 ml sweet chilli sauce
100 ml honey
125 ml lemon juice
15 ml Worcestershire sauce
15 ml chopped fresh marjoram
15 ml chopped fresh parsley
5 ml chopped fresh ginger

1   Cut the meat into 3 cm pieces. Thread alternately with the baby onions onto the skewers. Place in a shallow dish.
2   Combine all the marinade ingredients and pour over the kebabs. Place in the fridge overnight.
3   Drain off the excess marinade and cook the kebabs over hot coals for 6–8 minutes or until cooked to your liking.


# Surprise Beef Parcels

Serves 6

6 steaks (fillet, lazy-aged rump or rib-eye)
10 ml garlic
30 ml soy sauce
30 ml olive oil
1 x 40 g packet onion or mushroom soup

180 ml rosé wine
1 red onion, sliced
sprigs fresh thyme
freshly ground black pepper

1   Rub the steaks with the garlic and drizzle with the soy sauce and olive oil. Set aside, covered, in the fridge for a few hours or overnight.
2   Place each steak on a square of foil large enough to enclose it completely. Sprinkle 10 ml soup mix over each steak and spoon over 30 ml wine. Top with a few slices of onion, a sprig of thyme and freshly ground black pepper. Seal the foil parcels tightly and place on the braai.
3   Cook for about 10 minutes or until the steak is cooked to your liking.

# Piquant T-bone Steaks

Serves 4

4 T-bone steaks

**MARINADE**

60 ml soy sauce

30 ml oyster sauce

15 ml hoisin sauce

15 ml brown sugar

15 ml sherry

5 ml crushed garlic

5 ml sunflower oil

1   Combine all the ingredients for the marinade in a shallow dish and mix well. Add the T-bones, cover and place in the fridge to marinate overnight.
2   Drain the steaks and reserve the marinade. Cook on the braai for about 5 minutes on each side, depending on the thickness of the meat, until the desired doneness. Baste occasionally with the reserved marinade.

# Beef Satay

Serves 4

500 g beef mince

30 ml grated ginger or 10 ml ground ginger

2 cloves garlic, crushed

1 onion, grated

160 ml fresh coriander

5 ml ground coriander

5 ml turmeric

5 ml chilli powder

2 ml ground cardamom

10 ml salt

freshly ground black pepper

8 wooden skewers, soaked in water for 30 minutes

**GLAZE**

15 ml chopped fresh ginger

5 ml chopped garlic

25 ml tamarind paste

25 ml honey

1   Place all the ingredients for the meat into a food processor and pulse until combined.
2   Divide into 8 portions. Wet the hands and shape each portion around a soaked skewer to form a sausage shape. Chill in the fridge until required.
3   For the glaze, combine all the ingredients and mix well.
4   Grill the meat over hot coals until cooked, brushing with the glaze.

*Piquant T-bone Steaks*

# Rosemary-infused Lamb Chops with Bean, Strawberry and Feta Salad
Serves 10

20 lamb chops
15 ml fresh rosemary, chopped
150 ml olive oil
2 lemons, thinly sliced
1 bunch fresh mint, chopped
1 kg French beans, trimmed and blanched
1 large punnet fresh strawberries, sliced into quarters
400 g feta, cubed

**DRESSING**
125 ml olive oil
100 ml red wine or raspberry vinegar
20 ml water
2 cloves garlic, crushed
15 ml castor sugar
5 ml Dijon mustard

1  Rub the lamb chops with salt and rosemary. Place in a shallow dish and pour over the olive oil. Add the lemon slices and half of the mint. Toss to coat and allow to marinate for 1 hour.
2  Combine all the dressing ingredients and set aside.
3  Place the chops over the coals and cook to your liking.
4  Just before serving, combine the remaining mint with the beans, strawberries and feta. Pour the dressing over the bean and strawberry mixture. Place on a large platter, toss lightly and top with the chops. Serve immediately.

# Lamb Steaks with Lemon and Rosemary
Serves 4

juice and rind of 1 large lemon
60 ml olive oil
2 cloves garlic, chopped

30 ml chopped fresh rosemary
salt and freshly ground black pepper
750 g lamb steaks or chops

1  Combine all the ingredients except the meat and mix well. Place the meat in the mixture for a few hours or overnight.
2  Cook the meat over a high heat for 4–5 minutes on each side until cooked to desired doneness. Baste with the marinade during cooking.

*Rosemary-infused Lamb Chops with Bean, Strawberry and Feta Salad*

# Lamb Chops with Mediterranean Marinade
Serves 4

60 ml olive oil

3 cloves garlic, chopped

50 ml chopped fresh coriander

45 ml tomato paste

15 ml honey

10 ml Dijon mustard

5 ml ground paprika

10 ml ground cumin

pinch saffron (optional)

salt and freshly ground black pepper

1 kg lamb chops

1  Combine all the ingredients except the meat and mix well. Marinate the meat in the mixture for a few hours or overnight.
2  Remove the meat from the marinade and cook over a medium-high heat for 4–5 minutes on each side, basting with the marinade until cooked.


# Devilled Lamb Chops
Serves 4

30 ml olive oil

30 ml runny honey

30 ml French mustard

30 ml Worcestershire sauce

3–5 ml chilli flakes

3 ml cayenne pepper

8 lamb chops or steaks

1  Combine all the ingredients except the meat.
2  Pour over the lamb and marinate for at least 30 minutes.
3  Remove from the marinade and cook chops over the coals for 10–12 minutes, turning and basting frequently with the reserved marinade. (Steaks may need less cooking time; see page 13.)
4  Serve with Chickpea Couscous.


# Chickpea Couscous
Serves 4

100 g instant couscous, cooked according to the
   package instructions

1 x 400 g can chickpeas, well drained and rinsed

1 small red onion, finely sliced

5 Peppadews™, finely sliced

30 ml finely chopped fresh mint

30 ml finely chopped fresh coriander

**DRESSING**

30 ml olive oil

30 ml lemon juice

3 ml ground cumin

salt and freshly ground black pepper

1  Combine the couscous with the chickpeas, onion, Peppadews™, mint and coriander.
2  Combine all the ingredients for the dressing, pour over the couscous and toss gently. Serve with the devilled lamb chops or steaks.

*Devilled Lamb Chops with Chickpea Couscous*

# Greek Lamb and Feta Burgers
Serves 4

2 slices stale bread, crusts removed, grated

500 g lamb mince

1 onion, grated

5 ml ground cumin

5 ml ground coriander

45 ml flat-leaf parsley, finely chopped

salt and freshly ground black pepper

200 g feta cheese, drained

15 ml olive oil

4 hamburger rolls or pita breads

mint leaves

tomato relish

1  Combine the bread, mince, onion, spices, parsley and seasoning.
2  Wet the hands, divide the mixture into four and shape each into a burger patty. Make a hollow in each patty and fill with a quarter of the feta cheese, then reshape the patty.
3  Cover with clingfilm and refrigerate for 1 hour.
4  Cook the patties over gentle coals for approximately 10 minutes, ensuring they are cooked through.
5  Serve in bread rolls with mint leaves and tomato relish.


# Moroccan Spiced Lamb
Serves 4–6

1 butterflied leg of lamb, ±900 g

30 ml Moroccan spice

60 ml lemon juice

80 ml olive oil

3 cloves garlic, chopped

1  Open out the leg of lamb and flatten for even thickness.
2  Combine the remaining ingredients. Place the lamb into a plastic bag and pour over the marinade. Rub well into the meat. Leave to marinate for 4 hours or overnight.
3  Remove from the marinade and cook for 5 minutes on each side over high heat. Continue cooking for ± 30 minutes over medium heat, basting with the remaining marinade. Leave the meat to rest for 10 minutes before slicing.

*Greek Lamb and Feta Burgers*

# Marinated Grilled Lamb with Hummus, Olive Oil and Coriander

Serves 6–8

12 lamb chops

30 ml olive oil

45 ml balsamic vinegar

3 dried chillies, crumbled

5 ml crushed coriander seeds

2.5 ml ground cumin

2.5 ml ground ginger

juice of 1 lemon

freshly ground black pepper

1 onion, peeled and cut into rings

**HUMMUS**

1 x 400 g can of chickpeas, drained and rinsed

juice of 1 lemon

1 large garlic clove, peeled and crushed

15 ml tahini (sesame seed paste)

±100 ml olive oil

salt

a dash of Tabasco® sauce

2.5 ml ground cumin

**GARNISH**

a small bunch fresh coriander

olive oil

lemon wedges

1   Place the lamb chops in a shallow dish. Mix together all the other ingredients, except the onion, to make a marinade. Pour over the chops and mix well until evenly coated. Tuck in the onion rings among the chops, cover with clingfilm and marinate for at least 12 hours or overnight.

2   To make the hummus, place the chickpeas in a food processor together with the lemon juice, garlic, tahini and a little water. Pulse to form a paste. Pour in the olive oil in a thin stream. Add more or less than the specified olive oil, depending on how creamy you want the hummus. Season with the salt, Tabasco® sauce and cumin, spoon into a bowl and set aside.

3   Sprinkle the chops with salt and cook over medium coals or on a preheated gas braai. Cook on both sides until brown and crispy, and preferably still pink in the middle. For well-done chops, cook for longer.

4   To serve, place a swirl of hummus in the centre of each plate and top with two chops and a few sprigs of fresh coriander. Drizzle with the olive oil and serve with the lemon wedges.

*Marinated Grilled Lamb with Hummus, Olive Oil and Coriander and Grilled Pear, Asparagus and Rocket Salad (page 138)*

*Roast Leg of Lamb*

# Rosemary Lamb Kebabs
Serves 4

500 g lamb, cubed

2 cloves garlic, crushed

30 ml soy sauce

45 ml medium sherry or white wine

5 ml prepared coarse mustard

salt and freshly ground black pepper

cocktail tomatoes

6–8 fresh rosemary twigs, stripped, but with a few
leaves remaining on one end

1 Place the lamb in a bowl. Add the garlic, soy sauce, sherry or wine, mustard and seasoning. Leave to stand, covered, for 2 hours or refrigerate overnight.
2 Remove the lamb from the marinade and pierce each cube with a sharp knife for easy assembly onto the rosemary twigs. Thread onto the rosemary twigs alternately with the cocktail tomatoes. Use three lamb cubes and two tomatoes per kebab.
3 Place over medium coals and cook for 3–5 minutes on each side, basting frequently with the remaining marinade.

# Roast Leg of Lamb
Serves 6–8

1 large leg of lamb

**MARINADE**

1 litre red or white wine

6 cloves garlic, crushed

1 large onion, cut into rings

4 twigs fresh rosemary

15 black peppercorns

6 juniper berries

**SEASONING**

30 ml olive oil

30 ml butter

30 ml balsamic vinegar

30 ml fresh rosemary, lightly crushed

30 ml ready-made whole grain mustard

3 cloves garlic, crushed

2 red chillies, seeded and chopped

salt and freshly ground black pepper

1 Combine all the marinade ingredients. Place the lamb in a non-metal or earthenware dish. Pour over the marinade and leave covered in the fridge overnight or for up to 24 hours.
2 Remove the meat and set the marinade aside.
3 Mix together all the ingredients for the seasoning. Using a sharp knife, cut slits into the lamb at regular intervals. Rub the seasoning into the slits, then rub the remaining mixture over the entire leg.
4 Place the lamb on a grid over a metal or foil tray and cook over an indirect fire for 2–3 hours, replenishing the coals as needed. Baste the meat occasionally with the marinade.
5 Remove the lamb, cover with foil and leave to stand for 10–15 minutes before slicing. Strain the remaining marinade into a small saucepan and bring to the boil, thickening if necessary with a little cornflour or gravy powder. Serve alongside the meat.

# Vietnamese Lamb Parcels in Vine Leaves

Serves 4–6 as a starter

1 red onion, roughly chopped

1 stalk lemon grass

3 cloves garlic

10 ml chopped ginger

1 long red chilli, seeded and roughly chopped

30 ml fresh mint

30 ml fresh coriander

5 ml ground cumin

5 ml ground coriander

500 g lamb mince

15 ml Vietnamese or Thai fish sauce

15 ml light soy sauce

32–48 vine leaves

8–12 wooden skewers, soaked in water for
    30 minutes

1 lemon, cut into wedges

1   Place the onion, lemon grass, garlic, ginger, chilli, herbs and spices into a mini chopper and chop until fine. Alternatively, chop the ingredients finely by hand and mix together.

2   Add to the mince and mix well. Add the fish and soy sauces to the mixture. Rinse the vine leaves, then cover with boiling water. Leave the leaves in the water and take them out as you need them. They are not dried before using.

3   Place a vine leaf on your work surface, then place a mound of the mince mixture at the base. Roll up the leaf, folding in the sides, to form a neat, tight roll. Repeat with the other leaves. Thread 4 leaf rolls onto a soaked skewer and cook over direct heat for about 5 minutes per side depending on the size of the rolls. Remove and serve with a squeeze of lemon.

**Note:** Vine leaves are available bottled or vacuum-sealed in brine. They need to be rinsed well before using to get rid of the saltiness. If you have a grapevine, pick young leaves and freeze them in plastic bags. Before use, pour boiling water over the leaves.

# Butterflied Buttermilk Lamb and Green Peppercorn Marinade

Serves 6

1 butterflied leg of lamb

**MARINADE**

500 ml buttermilk

45 ml green peppercorns

15 ml chopped fresh rosemary

60 ml chopped fresh mint

2 cloves garlic, crushed

**TOPPING**

30 ml Dijon mustard

5 ml coarse salt

a small handful fresh rosemary leaves, chopped

1   In a dish large enough to hold the lamb, combine all the marinade ingredients. Add the lamb and rub the marinade into the meat. Cover and refrigerate for 12–24 hours.

2   Pour off the marinade and pat the meat dry with paper towel.

3   Combine the topping ingredients and rub over the lamb. Place the meat over indirect heat and cook for 40–50 minutes. Rest for 15 minutes covered with foil before slicing.

*Vietnamese Lamb Parcels in Vine Leaves*

## Lip-smacking Ribs
Serves 4

60 ml soft brown sugar

80 ml soy sauce

60 ml sweet chilli sauce

30 ml black bean sauce

80 ml tomato sauce

1 kg pork ribs, cut into pieces

1 Combine all the ingredients except the ribs and mix well. Pour the sauce over the ribs and marinate for 4 hours or overnight.
2 Remove the ribs from the marinade and cook over medium-high heat for about 15–20 minutes, turning frequently and brushing with the remaining marinade.

## Chinese Barbecue Pork
Serves 4

2 cloves garlic, crushed

25 ml chopped fresh ginger

50 ml soy sauce

50 ml sherry

45 ml soft brown sugar

30 ml hoisin sauce

15 ml peanut oil

50 ml runny honey

2 x 500 g pork fillets

1 Combine all the ingredients except the fillets. Marinate the meat in the sauce for 3–4 hours.
2 Remove the meat from the marinade and cook over a medium-high heat for about 20–30 minutes, basting with the sauce until the meat is cooked. Boil the remaining marinade in a saucepan for 3–5 minutes and serve with the meat.

## Rosemary Pork Chops
Serves 6

10 ml coarse salt

15 ml lightly crushed fresh rosemary leaves

1–2 garlic cloves, crushed

olive oil

6 pork loin chops

1 Combine the salt, rosemary and garlic in a mortar and pestle, moistening slightly with a splash of olive oil, then crush. Divide the mixture among the chops, then rub it in, massaging the meat.
2 Leave to stand for 15 minutes before cooking over high heat for 5–8 minutes on each side. Baste if necessary with olive oil. Serve with new potatoes.

*Lip-smacking Ribs, Grilled Baby Marrows and Brinjals (page 113)*
*and Oriental Cabbage Salad (page 133)*

*Pork Chops with Spice Rub and Orange and Ginger Sauce and Ginger Noodle Salad (page 143)*

# Pork Chops with Spice Rub and Orange and Ginger Sauce

*This recipe also works well with rump or porterhouse steak*

Serves 6

6 pork chops

**SPICE RUB**

30 ml ground coriander

20 ml five-spice powder

5 ml ground fennel seeds

2 ml ground ginger

10 ml hot chilli powder

2 ml freshly ground black pepper

2 ml ground cinnamon

30 ml coarse salt

15 ml brown sugar

**ORANGE AND GINGER SAUCE**

45 ml sesame oil

15 ml chopped fresh ginger

15 ml chopped fresh garlic

80 ml orange juice

2 ml five-spice powder

2 ml red chilli flakes

2 ml ground fennel seeds

30 ml balsamic vinegar

30 ml soy sauce

15 ml sugar

1  For the spice rub, thoroughly blend all the spices with the salt and brown sugar in a bowl, then set aside. Store well sealed in a cool, dry place; the mix will last for a few months.

2  For the orange and ginger sauce, whisk together all the ingredients in a small mixing bowl. The sauce will keep for 3 or 4 days in the fridge.

3  Rub the chops generously with the spice mixture and set aside for about 1 hour. Cook the chops over a medium-high heat until done. Serve with the sauce.


# Mango and Lemon Grass Pork Kebabs

Serves 4

500 g pork fillet, cut into 1 cm thick slices

2 large ripe, firm mangoes, peeled and cut into chunks

2 stalks lemon grass, cut into 3 cm lengths

30 ml palm sugar, grated (can use brown sugar instead)

60 ml fresh lime juice

30 ml fish sauce

15 ml olive oil

6 wooden skewers, soaked in water for 30 minutes

1  Thread the pork, mango and lemon grass alternately onto the skewers.

2  Place the kebabs in a large dish so that each one lies flat. Whisk together the palm sugar, lime juice, fish sauce and oil until the sugar dissolves. Pour over the kebabs and leave to marinate for at least 2 hours.

3  Remove from the marinade and cook over hot coals for about 5 minutes on each side. Turn and baste frequently with the remaining marinade and ensure that the pork cooks through without burning. Serve immediately.

# Apple Cider Pork Steaks
Serves 4

6–8 boneless pork steaks

15 ml olive oil

15 ml grated fresh ginger

10 ml soy sauce

350 ml apple cider

3 Granny Smith apples, cored and cut into wedges

1  In a container large enough in which to lay out the steaks, combine the olive oil, ginger, soy sauce and apple cider. Add the pork steaks and apple wedges. Marinate for at least 1 hour.
2  Remove the steaks and apple wedges from the marinade, and cook both over the coals for 5–8 minutes on each side. Baste frequently with the remaining marinade and ensure that the apple wedges do not burn, as they will cook more quickly than the steaks.
3  Serve the steaks with the apple wedges.


# Oriental Roast Pork Belly
Serves 4–6

1 pork belly

water to cover

1 onion, studded with 5 cloves

1 bay leaf

**MARINADE**

20 ml freshly grated ginger

2–3 garlic cloves, crushed

1 dried chilli, crumbled

100 ml soy sauce

45 ml brown sugar

15 ml fish sauce

1  Place the pork belly in a pot and pour over water to cover. Add the onion and bay leaf. Bring to the boil and simmer for 10–15 minutes.
2  While the pork is cooking, combine all the marinade ingredients and place in a dish large enough to hold the pork belly. Remove the pork from the water and place in the marinade. Toss to coat, then leave to stand for 1 hour, turning frequently.
3  Place over medium-hot coals, fat side up and cook for 15–20 minutes. Turn and cook for a further 10–15 minutes, basting frequently with the marinade. Finish off the cooking fat side up, ensuring that the fat is crispy and the meat is cooked through.

*Apple Cider Pork Steaks*

# Game

## Venison and Apricot Kebabs
Serves 6–8

1.5–2 kg fillet of venison, cubed
250 g thick bacon cubes

dried apricots, soaked in fruit juice
8 wooden skewers, soaked in water for 30 minutes

MARINADE
15 ml oil
2 large onions, chopped
20 ml curry powder
5 ml turmeric
10 ml ground coriander
15 ml smooth apricot jam
15 ml flour
500 ml vinegar
5 ml salt
3 bay leaves
freshly ground black pepper to taste

1 To prepare the marinade, heat the oil in a saucepan and fry the onions until softened. Add the curry powder, turmeric and ground coriander and fry gently, stirring. Stir in the remaining ingredients and simmer for a few minutes, then cool.
2 Thread the fillet cubes, apricots and bacon alternately onto skewers. Place in an oblong casserole dish and pour the marinade over. Leave to marinate overnight.
3 Cook over medium coals for about 15 minutes, or until cooked to desired doneness. Place the remaining marinade in a saucepan and bring to the boil. Serve with the kebabs.

## Teriyaki Ostrich Steaks
Serves 4

125 ml teriyaki sauce
60 ml orange juice
30 ml honey
15 ml chopped fresh ginger

10 ml chopped garlic
15 ml sesame oil
500 g ostrich fillet steaks

1 Combine all the ingredients for the marinade and marinate the steaks for 3–4 hours or overnight.
2 Remove the meat from the marinade. Cook over a high heat for about 4 minutes on each side, depending on the thickness of the steaks, until medium rare, basting with the marinade. Any remaining marinade can be boiled gently and served with the meat.

*Teriyaki Ostrich Steaks and Cracked Pepper and Cranberry Bread (page 125)*

*Ostrich Kebabs with Flat Bread*

# Ostrich Kebabs with Flatbread

Serves 4–6

1 kg ostrich steak, cubed
1 red onion, cut into wedges
1 red pepper, cut into 2 cm pieces
10 wooden skewers, soaked in water for
   30 minutes

**FLAT BREAD**
375 ml flour
10 ml sugar
180 ml boiling water

**MARINADE**
30 ml soy sauce
30 ml brown sugar
25 ml honey
30 ml sherry
25 ml hoisin sauce
10 ml chopped ginger
5 ml crushed garlic

1  Combine all the ingredients for the marinade and mix well. Add the ostrich and marinate for a few hours.
2  Meanwhile, prepare the flat bread. Combine the flour and sugar in a bowl, stir in the water quickly and mix well. Knead until the dough is smooth. Cover and leave to stand for about 30 minutes.
3  Divide the dough into 12 balls and roll each one into a thin round.
4  Fry in a dry, non-stick frying pan or on a braai griddle, until light brown on both sides. Keep covered with a clean dishcloth.
5  Drain the meat and thread alternately with onions and peppers onto the soaked skewers.
6  Cook over hot coals for about 8 minutes or until desired doneness. Serve with the flat bread.


# Ostrich Steaks with Juniper Rub

Serves 4

12 juniper berries
15 ml black peppercorns
30 ml coriander seeds

10 ml salt
500 g ostrich steaks

1  Combine all the seeds and the salt in a mortar and pestle, and pound until fine. Rub the steaks generously with the mixture and set aside for at least 30 minutes.
2  Cook the steaks on a hot griddle for 2–3 minutes on each side until cooked to desired doneness.
3  Delicious served with a ready-made Oriental plum sauce.

# Ostrich Sausage with Red Onion Relish

Serves 4

500 g ostrich sausage

**RELISH**

25 ml olive oil

3 large red onions, sliced

160 ml red wine

45 ml red wine vinegar

60 ml brown sugar

a few sprigs thyme

salt and freshly ground black pepper

1  Cook the sausage over hot coals until cooked through.
2  To prepare the relish, heat the oil and gently fry the onions for about 10 minutes. Add the remaining ingredients and cook gently until the mixture is reduced and thickened.
3  Serve with the cooked sausage.


# Smoked Ostrich Fillet with Cumberland Sauce

Serves 6

1 kg ostrich fillet steaks

30 ml olive oil

10 ml salt

10 ml ground ginger

7.5 ml brown sugar

5 ml freshly ground black pepper

45 ml brandied oak smoker dust

**CUMBERLAND SAUCE**

1 x 125 g jar redcurrant jelly (or use smooth apricot jam)

grated rind and juice of 1 large orange

grated rind and juice of 1 large lemon

125 ml red wine

1  Brush the meat with the olive oil.
2  Combine the salt, ginger, brown sugar and black pepper. Sprinkle this mixture over the meat.
3  Pour the flavoured smoker dust into a metal tray or foil container and place in a kettle braai over indirect heat.
4  Spread out the steaks over the grid. Cover with the lid and cook for 10–15 minutes according to preferred doneness.
5  To make the sauce, place all the ingredients in a saucepan and cook over low heat to dissolve the jelly. Serve hot or cold with the meat.

*Ostrich Sausage with Red Onion Relish and Garlic and Potato and Rosemary Pot Bread (page 118)*

*Venison Patties and Ratatouille (page 110)*

# Venison Patties

Serves 6

500 g venison mince
150 g bacon bits
5 ml salt
freshly ground black pepper
8 coriander seeds

2 allspice berries
pinch thyme
3 ml grated nutmeg
olive oil

1 Combine the mince and bacon bits.
2 Place the salt, pepper, coriander, allspice, thyme and nutmeg in a mortar and pestle, and pound until fine. Add to mince mixture and mix.
3 Shape into six patties. Cover and refrigerate for at least 1 hour.
4 Rub each patty with olive oil and cook over hot coals for 3–4 minutes on each side.

# Venison Potjie

Serves 10

3 kg venison chunks or ostrich neck, on bone
60 ml oil
3 large onions, sliced
500 g carrots, sliced
4 x 400 g cans whole peeled tomatoes
2–3 cloves garlic, crushed
1 large handful fresh rosemary or mixture of
   chives and parsley

30 ml sugar
15 ml salt
1 large bunch soup celery, chopped
300 ml red wine
2 x 400 g cans butter or cannellini beans,
   well drained
juice of 1 large lemon
freshly ground black pepper to taste

1 Brown the meat in hot oil in a potjie.
2 Remove the meat, then fry the onions and carrots, adding more oil if necessary.
3 Return the meat to the pot with the tomatoes, garlic, herbs, sugar, salt, celery and wine. Cover with foil, shiny side down, and cover with the lid. Cook for 3–4 hours, stirring once or twice. Don't be tempted to stir it too often. Add the beans, lemon juice and pepper, and cook for about 15 minutes until heated through. Check the seasoning.

# Poultry

# Chicken

## Chicken Tikka Kebabs
Serves 4

60 ml tikka paste

125 ml plain yoghurt

8 chicken breast fillets, cubed

1 red onion, cut into wedges (optional)

8 wooden skewers, soaked in water for 30 minutes

1  Combine the tikka paste and yoghurt, add the chicken and marinate, covered, in the fridge for 4 hours or overnight.
2  Remove the chicken from the marinade and thread onto the soaked skewers, alternating with the onion wedges, if desired.
3  Cook over medium-high heat for about 10 minutes, turning frequently. Serve with apple and mint sauce.

## Apple and mint sauce

1 green apple, peeled and grated

60 ml plain yoghurt

45 ml chopped fresh mint

15 ml lemon juice

salt and freshly ground black pepper

Combine all the ingredients and mix well.

## Mango Chutney Drumsticks
Serves 4

45 ml tomato sauce

10 ml Worcestershire sauce

45 ml mango chutney

15 ml honey

15 ml olive oil

6–8 drumsticks

1  Combine all the ingredients except the drumsticks and mix well.
2  Slash the flesh of the drumsticks to allow the flavour of the sauce to penetrate and also to cook more quickly. Marinate the drumsticks overnight.
3  Remove from the marinade and cook over a medium heat for 10–15 minutes, turning frequently, until cooked through. Baste with the leftover marinade.

*Chicken Tikka Kebabs, Portuguese-style Chicken Thighs (page 64)*
*and Carrot and Baby Marrow Salad (page 138)*

*Lime and Coriander Chicken with Avocado Sauce and Pasta Rice Salad (page 133)*

# Lime and Coriander Chicken

Serves 4

6–8 chicken breast fillets

100 ml lime juice

80 ml olive oil

2 cloves garlic, chopped

15 ml honey

60 ml chopped fresh coriander

1  Flatten the chicken breasts so that they are of equal thickness – this helps them to cook evenly.
2  Combine all the remaining ingredients and marinate the chicken, covered, in the fridge for 4 hours or overnight.
3  Remove from the marinade and cook over a high heat for 4–5 minutes on each side, brushing with any remaining marinade. Delicious served with avocado sauce.

## Avocado Sauce

1 ripe avocado, mashed

15 ml lemon juice

45 ml mayonnaise

30 ml chopped fresh coriander

4 spring onions, finely chopped

salt and freshly ground black pepper to taste

Mix all the ingredients well and season to taste.

# Cajun-spiced Spatchcock Chicken

Serves 4

3 cloves garlic, chopped

30 ml paprika

10 ml ground cinnamon

10 ml ground fennel

5 ml chilli powder

10 ml salt

10 ml ground coriander

5 ml ground cumin

10 ml dried origanum

45 ml olive oil

1 chicken, spatchcocked (flattened)

1  Combine the garlic, spices and herbs with the olive oil and rub into the chicken. Leave to stand for a few hours for the flavours to penetrate.
2  Cook the chicken over indirect heat for about 1 hour until cooked through.

# Hawker Chicken
Serves 4

8 chicken portions
olive oil

SPICES
5 ml each whole cardamom, black and yellow
    mustard seeds, fennel and coriander
2.5 ml turmeric
5 ml salt

1. Rub the chicken pieces with olive oil.
2. Place the whole spices in a mortar and pestle or spice mill, and grind until smooth. Add the turmeric and salt, and mix. Roll the chicken in the spices and place in a greased glass ovenproof dish. Cover and leave to stand in the fridge for 1 hour.
3. For a better end product, pre-cook the chicken in the microwave on high for 10 minutes. Transfer to the coals and cook, turning once, for 5–8 minutes on each side, taking care not to burn the outside of the chicken. Leave to stand for a couple of minutes before serving. Serve with bulgur pilaf.

# Bulgur Pilaf
Serves 4–6

250 ml bulgur (cracked) wheat
15 ml oil
1 litre boiling water
5–10 ml salt

a handful flaked almonds, toasted
1 bunch spring onions, finely chopped
salt and freshly ground black pepper to taste

Toast the bulgur in the preheated oil in a large pan. Pour the boiling water over and add the salt. Cook until the water has evaporated. Mix in the rest of the ingredients, check the seasoning and serve with the Hawker Chicken.

# Portuguese-style Chicken Thighs
Serves 4

5 ml freshly ground black pepper
5 ml dried origanum
1–2 chillies, chopped
1 clove garlic, crushed

5 ml paprika
60 ml red wine vinegar
60 ml olive oil
8 chicken thighs, cut in half through the joint

1. Combine all the ingredients, except the chicken, and mix well. Rub into the chicken pieces and leave to marinate in the fridge, covered, for 1 hour.
2. Cook on the braai over medium coals for 5–8 minutes on each side, turning and basting frequently.

*Hawker Chicken, Bulgur Pilaf and Hummus, Carrot and Sesame Salad (page 142)*

*Buffalo Drumsticks*

# Chilli Chicken Thighs

Serves 4

8 chicken thighs
500 ml chicken stock

**MARINADE**
125 ml lemon juice
1–2 chillies, seeded and chopped

30 ml olive oil
10 ml sesame oil
30 ml soy sauce
30 ml honey
1 small onion, finely chopped
30 ml fresh coriander, chopped

1  Poach the chicken thighs in the stock for 10 minutes. Remove and cool, then slash the thighs.
2  Combine all the ingredients for the marinade and mix well. Rub into the chicken and leave to marinate for a few hours.
3  Cook on the braai over medium coals for 5 minutes per side, basting frequently with the marinade.


# Oriental Chicken Kebabs

Serves 4

4 chicken thighs
4 chicken drumsticks
4 wooden skewers, soaked in water for 30 minutes

**MARINADE**
3 cloves garlic, crushed
15 ml grated fresh ginger

1 stalk lemon grass, finely sliced
1 onion, finely chopped
15 ml red curry paste
handful of fresh coriander, finely chopped
60 ml fish sauce
200 ml coconut milk
salt and freshly ground black pepper

1  Thread a thigh and drumstick onto each skewer. Microwave, covered, on high for 5 minutes, then leave to cool.
2  For the marinade, combine ingredients in a dish large enough to hold the skewered chicken portions. Stir to mix and place the chicken in the marinade, ensuring it is well coated. Cover and refrigerate for at least 1 hour, turning the chicken in the marinade a couple of times.
3  Remove from marinade. Cook for 5 minutes each side over hot coals. Turn and baste frequently.


# Buffalo Drumsticks

Serves 4

8 chicken drumsticks
500 ml chicken stock
1 clove garlic, crushed
125 ml tomato sauce

30 ml Worcestershire sauce
60 ml chutney
salt and freshly ground black pepper

1  Poach the chicken in the stock for 10 minutes. Remove and cool.
2  Combine the remaining ingredients and mix well. Add the chicken and marinate, covered, in the fridge for 3 hours.
3  Braai for 5 minutes on each side over medium coals, basting and turning frequently.

# Honey Mustard Chicken

Serves 4

4 chicken drumsticks, slashed three times on the
fleshy part

4 chicken thighs, slashed three times on the
fleshy part

**MARINADE**

2–3 cloves garlic, crushed

50 ml runny honey

30 ml whole grain mustard

30 ml soy sauce

15 ml lemon juice

freshly ground black pepper

1  Combine all the ingredients for the marinade in a large glass mixing bowl. Add the chicken and
stir to coat evenly with the marinade. Cover and refrigerate for at least 1 hour before cooking.

2  Just before placing on the braai, pre-cook the chicken in the microwave, covered, on high for
5 minutes, stirring halfway.

3  Place over medium coals and cook for 5 minutes on each side, turning and basting frequently.


# Tandoori Chicken

Serves 4

4 chicken drumsticks

4 chicken thighs

**MARINADE**

200 ml plain yoghurt

5 ml turmeric

5 ml ground coriander

5 ml ground cardamom

5 ml paprika

10 ml garam masala

1–2 cloves garlic, crushed

10 ml grated fresh ginger

salt and freshly ground black pepper

1  Slash the chicken pieces with a sharp knife.

2  Combine all the marinade ingredients in a large mixing bowl, add the chicken and mix to coat.
Cover and refrigerate for 1–2 hours or overnight.

3  Before cooking over the braai, place the chicken pieces on a baking tray and bake in a preheated
oven at 160 °C for 20 minutes, turning once.

4  Place over medium coals and cook for 5 minutes on each side, basting frequently with
the marinade.

*Honey Mustard Chicken and Pasta Salad with Herb Dressing (page 134)*

*Mediterranean Chicken Burgers*

# Chicken or Beef Satay

Serves 4–6

5 ml whole cumin
5 ml whole coriander
10 ml curry powder
10 ml turmeric
5 ml salt
45 ml oil
10 ml chopped fresh ginger

30 ml soy sauce
20 ml sugar
200 ml coconut milk
½ bunch fresh coriander, chopped
700 g chicken fillet strips or beef strips
18 wooden skewers, soaked in water for 30 minutes

1   Combine the cumin and coriander in a small saucepan and dry-fry over medium heat until fragrant.
2   Place the seeds in a mortar and pestle or coffee grinder, and grind to a powder. Combine with all the remaining ingredients to make a marinade. Add the chicken or beef strips and marinate, covered, in the fridge for a few hours or overnight if possible.
3   Thread the strips lengthwise onto the soaked wooden skewers and cook on a lightly oiled braai grid over hot coals for about 5 minutes, turning after 3 minutes. Serve hot with peanut sauce.

## Peanut Sauce

10 ml oil
½ small onion, finely chopped
10 ml chopped garlic
5 ml green curry paste
200 ml coconut milk

15 ml sugar
80 ml ground unsalted roasted peanuts
30 ml smooth peanut butter
10 ml soy sauce
15 ml lime or lemon juice

1   Heat the oil in a small, non-stick saucepan and fry the onion until soft. Add the garlic and curry paste, and mix well.
2   Add the remaining ingredients and simmer gently, stirring occasionally until thickened. Serve at room temperature with the chicken or beef skewers.

# Mediterranean Chicken Burgers

Makes 8

500 g chicken mince
8 sun-dried tomatoes in oil, drained and chopped
10 ml garlic, crushed
45 ml finely grated Parmesan cheese
30 ml pine nuts, toasted and chopped

100 ml fresh breadcrumbs
1 egg, lightly beaten
30 ml chopped fresh basil
30 ml chopped fresh parsley
salt and freshly ground black pepper to taste

1   Place the chicken mince in a large bowl. Add the remaining ingredients and season well with the salt and freshly ground black pepper.
2   With wet hands, shape the mixture into eight hamburger patties and place in the fridge to chill for 30 minutes.
3   Cook over medium coals for about 5 minutes on each side or until nicely browned and cooked through.

# Rotisserie Chicken

Serves 4–6

| | |
|---|---|
| 1.5 kg whole chicken | **MARINADE** |
| 1 whole onion, peeled | 125 ml oil |
| 1 lemon, sliced | 30 ml honey |
| | 30 ml freshly squeezed lime juice |
| | 3 ml paprika |
| | salt and freshly ground black pepper |

1  Rinse the chicken and pat dry.
2  Place the onion and lemon inside the cavity. Combine all the marinade ingredients in a saucepan over medium heat. Heat until the honey has completely dissolved.
3  Prepare an indirect fire with the drip pan in place (see page 10). Place the chicken on a grid or a rotisserie over the drip pan. Baste with the marinade, cover and cook for 1–1¼ hour or until the chicken is cooked. Baste every 15 minutes with the marinade. When cooked, wrap in foil and leave to rest for 15 minutes until ready to carve.


# Barbecued Chicken Pieces

Serves 6–8

| | |
|---|---|
| 8–12 chicken portions | **MARINADE** |
| | 100 ml oil |
| | 1 onion, chopped |
| | 15 ml crushed garlic |
| | 500 ml beer or chicken stock |
| | 215 g can tomato purée |
| | 60 ml chutney |
| | 10 ml whole grain mustard |
| | 20 ml Worcestershire sauce |
| | 30 ml apricot jam |
| | 5 ml salt |
| | freshly ground black pepper |

1  Heat the oil in a large saucepan and fry the onion and garlic. Add the remaining ingredients and bring to the boil. Add the chicken portions, reduce the heat and simmer for 30 minutes.
2  Remove the chicken and place on the braai. Cook over medium coals for 15 minutes, basting occasionally with the marinade until the chicken is cooked through.

*Rotisserie Chicken and Asparagus wrapped in Parma Ham (page 102)*

Beer Can Chicken

# Beer Can Chicken

1 lemon, halved

30 ml dried mixed herbs

5 ml freshly ground black pepper

5 ml salt

15 ml olive oil

1.5 kg whole chicken, giblets removed

1 x 340 ml can beer

1 Prepare the kettle braai for indirect cooking and insert a drip tray.
2 Squeeze one half of the lemon into a small bowl and add the herbs, pepper, salt and oil. Rub this mixture onto the outside and the inside of the chicken. Insert the other half of the lemon into the cavity of the chicken.
3 Drink ⅓ of the beer, then carefully open the top of the can completely with a can opener. Place the chicken over the open can of beer so that the chicken sits upright and the drumsticks point downwards.
4 Balance the can and chicken on top of the braai grid over the middle section of the fire.
5 Cover with the lid and cook without opening for 1½ hours or until the internal temperature of the chicken reaches 82 °C in the thigh area or the juices run clear when pierced with a sharp knife.
6 Remove from the braai, discard the beer can and allow the chicken to rest for 10 minutes before serving.

# Rosemary-smoked Chicken
Serves 4–6

1.5 kg whole chicken, giblets removed

1 lemon, quartered

6 fresh bay leaves

3 large sprigs fresh rosemary

15 ml olive oil

salt and freshly ground black pepper

500 ml smoking chips, soaked in water

1 Prepare the kettle braai for indirect cooking.
2 Cut away any excess fat from the chicken and insert the lemon quarters, bay leaves and one sprig of rosemary into the chicken cavity. Tie the drumsticks together with string and rub the chicken all over with the olive oil. Season with the salt and pepper.
3 When the fire is ready, fill the drip tray half full with water and position the chicken on the lightly oiled grid above the drip tray.
4 Drain the wood chips and carefully add a handful to the coals. Cover with the lid and cook for about 1½ hours, adding a handful of chips every 20 minutes.
5 Add the remaining sprigs of fresh rosemary to the coals with the last handful of wood chips.
6 When the chicken is cooked, transfer it to a serving dish and leave it to stand for 10 minutes before carving.

# Turkey & Duck

## Moroccan Spiced Turkey Steaks
Serves 4

4 turkey breasts, filleted
juice of 1 lemon
100 ml olive oil

2 cloves garlic, chopped
15 ml Moroccan spice
salt and freshly ground black pepper

1  Butterfly the turkey breasts and flatten with a rolling pin.
2  Combine the remaining ingredients and rub well into the breasts. Leave to marinate in the fridge, covered, for a few hours.
3  Remove from the marinade and cook over a high heat for 2–3 minutes on each side.


## Festive Turkey on the Braai
*This is a very popular way of cooking the Christmas turkey. For one thing, it takes the heat out of the kitchen, and it frees up oven space to cook other dishes.*
Serves 6–8

1 x 4–5 kg turkey
500 g boerewors
1 bunch fresh thyme

1 lemon, quartered
250 g streaky bacon

1  Wash the turkey inside and out, then pat dry with paper towel.
2  Stuff the cavity with the boerewors, thyme and lemon. Secure the cavity with string or a skewer.
3  Cover the breast area with the bacon slices. Prepare an indirect-heat fire in the kettle braai and place the turkey onto the cooking grate, making sure there is a drip tray with water underneath. Cover with the lid, but leave the vents open.
4  Roast for 25 minutes per kg or until the juices run clear when a skewer is inserted into the thickest part of the turkey. When inserted into the bird, a meat thermometer should read 77 °C. A large turkey of 4 to 5 kg should take 2½ –3 hours to cook. To make sure the temperature remains constant throughout, replenish the fire at least once halfway through the cooking time. Remove the turkey from the fire, cover with foil and leave to stand for 15 minutes before carving.

*Moroccan Spiced Turkey Steaks with Grilled Baby Marrows*
*with Feta and Pine Nuts (page 130)*

*Spiced Duck Breasts with Plums and Foil-cooked Potatoes with an Asian Twist (page 102)*

# Duck Breast with Tamarind Orange Glaze

Serves 6

500 ml orange juice

60 ml brown sugar

60 ml soy sauce

15 ml tamarind juice (pour boiling water over half a
packet of tamarind pulp and allow to soak for
30 minutes before draining the liquid and using)

3 cloves garlic, crushed

1 red chilli, seeded and chopped

pinch of Chinese five-spice powder

grated rind of 1 orange

6 duck breasts

salt

chives to garnish

1   Boil together the orange juice and sugar in a pan over medium heat until reduced by half, stirring often. This will take about 12 minutes.
2   Add the soy sauce, tamarind juice, garlic, chilli and five-spice powder. Simmer over medium heat until reduced to approximately 125 ml.
3   Strain into a small pan and add the orange rind. Set aside.
4   Cut four slits into each duck breast and season generously with salt. Place skin-side up over medium coals and cook for 5 minutes using the indirect cooking method.
5   Turn and cook for a further 3–5 minutes or longer for preferred doneness.
6   Bring the glaze in the pan to the boil.
7   Slice each duck breast crosswise and fan on a serving plate. Drizzle with the glaze, garnish with the chives and serve.

# Spiced Duck Breasts with Plums

*Great to make when plums are plentiful*

Serves 4

4 duck breasts

10 ml Chinese five-spice powder

6–8 plums, stoned and quartered

1 clove garlic, chopped

60 ml soy sauce

30 ml cider vinegar

30 ml brown sugar

30 ml apricot jam

15 ml grated fresh ginger

30 ml honey

30 ml olive oil

1   Cut the skin of the duck breasts diagonally and rub in some of the five-spice powder. Leave to stand at room temperature for 1 hour.
2   In a saucepan, combine the plums with the remaining ingredients, except the honey and olive oil, and cook gently for 5–6 minutes until the plums are just tender.
3   When ready to cook over the coals, brush the duck breasts with a mixture of honey and olive oil and cook over medium coals for about 4 minutes on each side until medium rare.
4   When the duck is cooked, remove from the heat, slice each breast into 1 cm thick slices, pour over the plum mixture, and serve.

# Seafood

# Prawn, Avocado and Bacon Kebabs
Serves 4–6

1 firm, ripe avocado
30 ml lemon juice
salt and freshly ground black pepper
125 g streaky bacon
50 ml olive oil

15 ml soy sauce
1 clove garlic, crushed
300 g prawn tails
1 red onion, cut into wedges
wooden skewers, soaked in water for 30 minutes

1   Cut the avocado into cubes about 2 cm square, and sprinkle with a little of the lemon juice and salt and pepper.
2   Wrap each square in ½ slice bacon. Combine the remaining lemon juice, olive oil, soy sauce and garlic, and marinate the prawns for 20 minutes.
3   Thread the bacon-wrapped avocado, onion wedges and prawns alternately onto the skewers and cook over medium coals for about 5 minutes, turning frequently, until the bacon is cooked.

# Spicy Fish Burgers
Makes 4

500 g fresh fish (use 250 g Canadian salmon and
   250 g hake, or hake only)
1–2 red chillies, seeded and chopped
1 clove garlic, chopped
15 ml fish sauce
30 ml sweet chilli sauce
80 ml chopped fresh coriander
45 ml cornflour
1 egg
oil for brushing

**TO SERVE**
hamburger rolls
butter lettuce
slices red onion
1 tomato, sliced
½ cucumber, cut into ribbons with a potato peeler

1   Cut the fish into rough chunks and place into a food processor with all the remaining ingredients. Process well until the mixture forms a rough ball.
2   Remove and shape into four generous patties.
3   Refrigerate for 30 minutes to firm up.
4   When ready to cook, brush the patties with oil and cook on a heated griddle for 3–4 minutes on each side.
5   Serve on the hamburger rolls with the lettuce, onion slices, tomato and cucumber.

*Prawn, Avocado and Bacon Kebabs*

*Whole Braaied Line Fish with Ginger and Coriander*

# Calamari Tubes with Lemon and Chilli
Serves 4

500 g small calamari tubes

MARINADE

45 ml lemon juice

60 ml olive oil

1–2 red chillies, seeded and chopped

10 ml chopped garlic

1 stalk lemon grass, finely chopped (optional)

lemon wedges, for serving

Combine all the ingredients for the marinade and mix well. Add the calamari and marinate for 30 minutes. Cook the calamari on a skottel or flat griddle over a very high heat for 1–2 minutes on each side. Serve with the lemon wedges.

**HINT:** These tubes are also delicious when placed on top of a mixed salad and drizzled with olive oil and a squeeze of lemon.

# Whole Braaied Linefish with Ginger and Coriander
Serves 2

1 large linefish, about 1 kg (ask your fishmonger to
   clean and scale the fish)

80 ml peanut oil

15 ml sesame oil

15 ml soy sauce

juice of 2 lemons

30 ml rice vinegar

15 ml grated fresh ginger

80 ml chopped fresh coriander

salt and freshly ground black pepper

1   Cut slits in the flesh on both sides.
2   Mix the remaining ingredients and pour over the fish. Cover and refrigerate for 2–3 hours.
3   Remove the fish from the marinade and set the marinade aside.
4   Place the fish in a hinged fish holder (see page 6) and braai for 10–15 minutes on each side until done, basting with the reserved marinade, which has been brought to a gentle boil.

**HINT:** Depending on the size of the fish and the shape of your fish holder, you may need to remove the head before braaiing.

# Crumbed Braaied Whole Fish

*Crumbing the fish and braaiing it whole keeps it very moist*
Serves 2–4, depending on the size of the fish.

4 slices fresh white bread, crumbed

125 ml finely chopped fresh herbs (a mixture of dill and parsley is nice)

salt and freshly ground black pepper to taste

1 medium-sized whole linefish

45 ml flour, seasoned with salt and pepper

1 egg, beaten

30–40 ml olive oil

lemon wedges, for serving

1   Combine the breadcrumbs with the herbs and season generously.
2   Coat the fish in a layer of seasoned flour. Dip it into the beaten egg, then coat generously with the breadcrumb mixture. Place on a plate and refrigerate for at least 1 hour to allow the crumbs to settle onto the fish.
3   Place the fish into a hinged fish holder (see page 6), place over medium–hot coals and cook for 15–20 minutes on each side, depending on the size of the fish. Drizzle generously with the olive oil while cooking.
4   Remove from the heat, turn out onto a plate and serve with the lemon wedges. To test whether the fish is cooked, insert a fork into the thickest part to see if it flakes easily.

# Mussel Parcels with White Wine and Herbs

Serves 4

1.5 kg fresh mussels, well cleaned

250 ml dry white wine

juice and rind of 1 lemon

1 bunch spring onions, finely chopped

10 ml chopped fresh garlic

salt and freshly ground black pepper to taste

125 ml chopped fresh herbs (dill, basil or parsley)

1   Cut three large pieces of heavy-duty foil and place them on top of each other. Pile the mussels into the centre of the foil and add the remaining ingredients. Fold the foil over the mussels and seal.
2   Cook the mussels over a high heat until they have all opened – this will take about 10 minutes.
3   Discard any mussels that don't open or are damaged in any way. Divide the mussels and the liquid among four bowls, and serve with crusty bread to soak up all the juices.

*Mussel Parcels with White Wine and Herbs*

*Calamari Steaks*

# Fish Burgers
Serves 4–6

350 g potatoes, peeled and cut into chunks
2 egg yolks
50 ml butter
1 onion, finely chopped
500 g Cape whiting fillets, poached

500 ml fresh breadcrumbs
15 ml lemon juice
25 ml chopped fresh parsley
salt and freshly ground black pepper
50 ml oil

1  Cook the potatoes in salted boiling water. Drain and mash with the egg yolks.
2  Melt 25 ml of the butter in a frying pan and fry the onion until softened.
3  Finely flake the fish and combine with the potatoes, onion, breadcrumbs, lemon juice and parsley.
4  Season with salt and pepper and mix well.
5  Divide the mixture into 6 large patties. Cover and chill in the fridge until ready to cook. Brush the burgers on both sides with a little oil and cook over medium coals for about 5 minutes on each side until cooked. Serve with a salad or on hamburger rolls.

# Calamari Steaks
Serves 4

800 g calamari steaks

**MARINADE**
125 ml lemon juice
125 ml dry white wine

10 ml crushed garlic
10 ml chopped fresh dill
10 ml chopped fresh parsley
salt and freshly ground black pepper
2.5 ml paprika

1  Combine the ingredients for the marinade in a large bowl. Add the calamari and marinate for at least 1 hour.
2  Cook over medium coals for 3–4 minutes on each side, basting frequently with the marinade.

# Baked Linefish
Serves 2–4, depending on the size of the fish

1 whole linefish, gutted and scaled
1 bunch parsley
1 bunch dill
1 small fennel bulb, thinly sliced

1 lemon, cut into slices
a little olive oil
30 ml dry white wine
salt and freshly ground black pepper

1  Rinse the fish and pat dry with paper towel. Oil a large piece of foil and place half the herbs in the centre. Lay the fish on top and place the lemon slices and remaining herbs inside the fish. Drizzle with the olive oil and wine, and season with salt and pepper.
2  Seal the foil around the fish to form a parcel. Place the parcel on the braai over glowing coals and cook for 25–30 minutes or until the fish comes away from the bones easily.

# Tikka-style Fish

Serves 2–4, depending on the size of the fish

| | |
|---|---|
| 1 whole linefish | 30 ml olive oil |
| 10 ml grated root ginger | 10 ml turmeric |
| 20 ml crushed garlic | 10 ml mild chilli powder |
| 90 ml plain yoghurt | 15 ml cumin seeds |

1 Slash the skin of the fish with a sharp knife.
2 Mix the ginger and garlic, and rub all over the fish. Combine the yoghurt, oil and spices, and coat the fish inside and out with this mixture. Chill in the fridge for at least 30 minutes before cooking.
3 Cook directly on the rack or in foil over hot coals for 10 minutes on each side. The cooking time will depend on how big the fish is and how hot the braai is when you start cooking.


# Braaied Snoek with Apricot Glaze

Serves 2–4

| | |
|---|---|
| 1 side of snoek | **GLAZE** |
| freshly ground black pepper | 45 g butter |
| | 45 ml oil |
| | 15 ml smooth apricot jam |
| | 5 ml crushed garlic |
| | 15 ml lemon juice |

1 Place the snoek in an oiled, hinged braai grid and sprinkle with the pepper.
2 Combine the glaze ingredients in a small saucepan. Heat, stirring until smooth. Using a small brush, brush the fish with the glaze.
3 Braai over medium coals, skin side down, basting frequently, for about 25 minutes or until the fish comes off the grid easily (the skin may stay behind).
4 Serve immediately.

*Tikka-style Fish*

*Seafood Potjie*

# Newspaper-baked Linefish

Serves 2–4, depending on the size of the fish

1 large, whole, firm-fleshed linefish
50 ml lemon juice
50 ml olive oil
20–25 ml chopped fresh mixed herbs
60 ml chopped spring onion

1–2 tomatoes, sliced
1 small fennel bulb, chopped
salt and freshly ground black pepper

1   Season the fish cavity with half of the lemon juice and oil, the herbs and spring onion.
2   Fill the cavity with tomato and fennel. Secure with toothpicks.
3   Place on a large sheet of greaseproof paper and drizzle with the remaining olive oil and lemon juice. Fold up like a parcel. Wrap the fish securely in three large sheets of newspaper, and wet thoroughly under a cold tap.
4   Place the fish in a hollow in warm coals. Allow about 45 minutes cooking time. When the fish is done, the outer layers of the newspaper will be blackened. Remove the fish from the coals and carefully unwrap the newspaper and greaseproof paper. Serve immediately.

# Seafood Potjie

Serves 8–10

1 kg filleted, skinless fish (use any firm fish)
400 g headless prawns
4–5 crayfish tails
36 black mussels
400 g calamari rings or tubes, cut into rings
60 ml olive oil

2 onions, sliced
2 x 410 g cans chopped tomatoes
10–15 ml crushed garlic
5 ml turmeric
60 ml chopped fresh parsley
salt and freshly ground black pepper to taste

1   Cut the fish into large cubes.
2   De-vein the prawns and crayfish tails, and rinse the mussels well.
3   Heat the oil in a potjie and lightly brown the onions. Stir in the tomato, garlic, turmeric and half of the parsley. Cover and simmer for 5 minutes. Add the fish, crayfish and prawns, cover and simmer for 5 minutes. Add the calamari and mussels, and simmer for 2 minutes, adding some stock if necessary.
4   Cook until the calamari is opaque and the mussels have opened.
5   Season to taste and sprinkle over the remaining parsley. Serve immediately with crusty bread to mop up all the delicious juices.

# Seafood Paella made on the Skottel

Serves 8–10

6 chicken fillets

3 crayfish tails, split in half lengthwise and the
  alimentary canals discarded (the crayfish can
  be omitted if it is too expensive)

18 large prawns

80 ml olive oil

salt and freshly ground black pepper

3 onions, chopped

1 each green and red pepper, seeded and cut
  into strips

500 g uncooked rice

1.5 litres chicken stock

a large pinch saffron threads, soaked in 60 ml
  boiling water, or use 5 ml turmeric

3 cloves garlic, crushed

500 g calamari rings

500 g smoked ham, cubed

500 g chorizo sausage, sliced

4 ripe red tomatoes, peeled, seeded and chopped

500 g cooked peas

24 black half-shell mussels

1  Cut the chicken into chunks. Set aside.
2  Leaving the shells intact, chop each crayfish half-tail into two.
3  Slit the prawns down the backs of the shells and de-vein.
4  Heat the oil and brown the chicken pieces in batches. Set aside and season with salt and pepper. Fry the crayfish and prawns, then set aside with the chicken. Cook the onions and peppers until soft but not brown. Add the rice and cook, stirring, until the grains are transparent and the oil is absorbed. Add the stock, saffron or turmeric, garlic, salt and pepper, then add the calamari, ham, chorizo, tomatoes and peas in layers.
5  Bring the liquid to the boil and boil fairly rapidly for approximately 25–30 minutes until all the liquid has been absorbed and the rice is tender. Stir from time to time, especially when the paella starts cooking. Add more stock or white wine if the liquid evaporates before the rice is cooked.
6  Ten minutes before the end of cooking, add the chicken, crayfish tails, prawns and mussels to the top of the paella, but do not stir. Heat through. Serve with a green salad and crusty bread.

# Crayfish with Lime and Herbs

Serves 6

6 medium crayfish tails

80 ml olive oil

10 ml grated lime rind

125 ml freshly squeezed lime juice

2 cloves garlic, crushed

30 ml coarsely chopped fresh coriander

30 ml coarsely chopped fresh flat-leaf parsley

6 limes, cut into wedges

1  Remove and discard the soft shell on the underside of the crayfish tails to expose the flesh. Combine the oil, rind, lime juice, garlic, coriander and parsley in a large bowl, then add the crayfish and mix. Cover and refrigerate for 1 hour.
2  Drain the crayfish and reserve the marinade. Cook the crayfish on a heated, oiled braai grid, uncovered, until browned all over and cooked through. Brush occasionally with the reserved marinade. Serve with the lime wedges.

*Crayfsh wth Lime and Herbs*

*Lemon Pepper Sardines*

# Grilled Stuffed Masala Prawns with Mint Yoghurt

Serves 4

20 large prawns in the shell, de-veined

10 ml coriander seeds

3 ml black peppercorns

3 ml fennel seeds

30 ml ground almonds

2 spring onions, white parts only, cut into
   1 cm pieces

2 cloves garlic, peeled and chopped

2 slices fresh ginger, peeled and chopped

30 ml fresh dill, chopped

5 ml masala or curry powder

3 ml salt

oil for grilling

### MINT YOGHURT

30 ml fresh mint, finely chopped

3 ml ground cumin

3 ml ground coriander

175 ml plain yoghurt

30 ml mayonnaise

5 ml sugar

salt and white pepper

1 Using a sharp knife, cut along the side of the prawns where the vein has been removed and make a cavity for the stuffing.

2 Toast the coriander seeds, peppercorns, fennel seeds and almonds in a dry pan until golden and aromatic. Grind finely in a spice grinder or mortar and pestle. Mix together the spring onions, garlic and ginger, then add the dill, spicy nut paste, masala or curry powder and salt.

3 Press some of the mixture into the cavity of each prawn and smooth the surface. Set aside for 10 minutes before cooking.

4 Grill the prawns over hot coals in their shells for 3–4 minutes per side until they turn orange-red. Serve 5 prawns to each person together with small pots of mint yoghurt for dipping. For the mint yoghurt, whisk together all ingredients.

# Lemon Pepper Sardines

Serves 4 as a starter

12 sardines

### MARINADE

juice and rind of one large lemon

30 ml black peppercorns, toasted and crushed (use
   Szechwan peppercorns for Oriental flavour)

5 ml sea salt

30 ml olive oil

fresh basil, chopped

extra lemon juice, olive oil and freshly ground
   black pepper for serving

1 Slit open the belly of each fish. Remove the spine and bones from the flesh.

2 Combine all the ingredients for the marinade, pour over the sardines and leave to marinate for 1 hour.

3 Remove from the marinade and cook over medium coals for 2–3 minutes on each side. Serve with the extra lemon juice, olive oil and pepper. Mop up the juices with crusty bread.

# Charcoal-grilled Sardines

Serves 4

20–24 sardines (5–6 per person)                250 ml coarse salt

1   Wash the sardines but do not descale or gut them. Sprinkle with the coarse salt, arrange in layers in a large bowl and leave for 1 hour.
2   Tilt the bowl to pour off the brine and shake off any excess salt before grilling.
3   Place the sardines on the grid and cook on both sides over hot coals until golden – about 3–4 minutes per side. Serve with boiled or baked potatoes.


# Hot Smoked Side of Salmon

*A very simple but delicious way to prepare salmon on the kettle braai*
Serves 6

1 whole side of salmon (if a whole side is not        30 ml olive oil
   available, use two large fillets with the skin on)     smoking chips or flavoured wood to give a
salt and freshly ground black pepper                   smoked flavour

1   Prepare an indirect fire and let the coals burn down. Place the salmon onto an oiled, hinged fish holder (see page 6), skin side down, season with the salt and pepper, and brush with some of the olive oil.
2   Place the fish basket onto the grill rack with coals on either side, add the smoker chips or wood to the coals, close the lid and the vents, and cook for about 20 minutes, depending on the thickness of the salmon.
3   Remove and serve with lemon slices or wedges, or a good-quality mayonnaise.

*Hot Smoked Side of Salmon*

# Vegetables

# Foil-cooked Potatoes with an Asian Twist
Serves 4–6

4–6 potatoes, cut into 5 mm-thick slices

60 g butter

45 ml soy sauce

10 ml sesame oil

2 cloves garlic, finely chopped

1 bunch spring onions, finely chopped

30 ml sesame seeds

salt and freshly ground black pepper to taste

1   Cut 6 sheets of heavy-duty foil, each approximately 30 cm long. Place the foil shiny side down and spread some butter where the potatoes will be placed.
2   On each sheet, arrange the slices of one potato in a mound on top of the butter, and sprinkle with the remaining ingredients (divided amongst the 6 parcels). Seal the parcels well.
3   Cook over indirect heat, covered, for at least 30 minutes. Take care when opening the parcels, as hot steam will escape. Ring the changes and use flavoured butters in parcels as well as a variety of different spices.


# Grilled Sweetcorn with Coriander Butter
Serves 4

4 ears of sweetcorn, husks removed

olive oil for brushing

**CORIANDER BUTTER**

125 g butter

salt and freshly ground black pepper

1 clove garlic, chopped

grated rind and juice of 1 small lemon

125 ml chopped fresh coriander

1 red chilli, seeded and chopped

1   Rub the sweetcorn with some olive oil and cook over direct heat, turning frequently, for 8–12 minutes until cooked. Combine all the ingredients for the butter in a bowl and mix well.
2   Remove the sweetcorn from the heat and serve with the coriander butter.


# Asparagus wrapped in Parma Ham
*This is a delicious starter*
Serves 4

1 bunch asparagus, blanched

100 g Parma ham, thinly sliced

olive oil

salt and freshly ground black pepper

1   Trim the asparagus spears, rinse well and pat dry.
2   Wrap a bundle of asparagus in Parma ham. Brush with olive oil and cook over a medium heat until the Parma ham is crispy and the asparagus is just tender, taking care that the bundles do not burn.
3   Remove and season with salt and pepper. Increase the quantities to feed more people.

**NOTE:** This recipe also works well if you use streaky bacon instead of Parma ham.

*Grilled Sweetcorn with Coriander Butter*

*Grilled Mushrooms with Tomato Salsa and Avocado and Bacon Wraps (page 109)*

# Vegetarian Skewers
Serves 6

4–5 small baby marrows
4–5 baby brinjals
12–14 button mushrooms
1 red pepper
1 yellow pepper
1 red onion, cut into wedges and separated
12–14 cocktail tomatoes

60 ml lemon juice
100 ml olive oil
3 cloves garlic, crushed
60 ml chopped fresh Italian parsley
salt and freshly ground black pepper
6 wooden skewers, soaked in water for 30 minutes

1   Cut the baby marrows into 2 cm pieces. Leave the brinjals whole, if small, or cut in half. Cut the peppers into 2 cm cubes.
2   Place all the vegetables in a glass bowl. Combine the lemon juice, olive oil, garlic and parsley, and mix well. Pour over the vegetables and season well. Marinate for 30 minutes.
3   Thread the vegetables onto the skewers and cook over a high heat for 8–10 minutes, until the vegetables are just tender. Turn frequently and brush with the marinade.

# Grilled Mushrooms with Tomato Salsa
Serves 6

45 ml balsamic vinegar
45 ml olive oil
30 ml chopped fresh Italian parsley
2 cloves garlic, crushed
6 large brown mushrooms

SALSA
3 ripe red tomatoes (vine ripened are best), seeded
    and cut into small cubes
1 bunch spring onions, white parts only,
    finely chopped
a good handful fresh basil leaves, finely torn
200 g mozzarella cheese, cut into small cubes
salt and freshly ground black pepper
pinch sugar

1   Combine the balsamic vinegar, olive oil, parsley and garlic, and mix well.
2   Brush some of the mixture over the mushrooms and reserve the rest. Grill the mushrooms on the braai until just tender but still retaining their shape. Place onto a serving platter.
3   For the salsa, combine all the ingredients and pour over the reserved balsamic mixture. Pile onto the mushrooms. Delicious served with grilled Italian bread slices.

# Braaied Green Tomatoes
Serves 4

250 ml fresh breadcrumbs

1 large handful fresh coriander, chopped

30 ml Moroccan spice

30 ml sun-dried tomatoes in olive oil, drained and
finely chopped

4 green tomatoes

olive oil

**YOGHURT SAUCE**

250 ml thick plain yoghurt

½ small red onion, finely chopped

15 ml lemon juice

5 ml ground cumin

1 clove garlic, crushed

salt and freshly ground black pepper to taste

a handful of fresh mint leaves, lightly chopped

1  Combine the breadcrumbs, coriander, spice and sun-dried tomatoes.
2  Cut off the stalks and rounded ends of the tomatoes and slice in half horizontally so you have two thick slices per tomato. Brush generously with the olive oil. Divide the breadcrumb mixture among the 8 slices.
3  Place on a heated grill and cook for 5–8 minutes, without turning, until heated through.
4  For the yoghurt sauce, combine all the ingredients. Allow two tomato slices per person and serve with a dollop of yoghurt sauce and warm pita bread.


# Roast Garlic and Onion Parcels
Serves 4

4 large heads of garlic

4 large onions

4 whole cloves

sprigs of fresh rosemary

4 knobs butter

salt and freshly ground black pepper

olive oil

Slice the tops off the garlic bulbs. Peel the onions and stud each with a clove. Make up parcels using foil to enclose one head of garlic and one onion. Sprinkle with the rosemary, add a knob of butter and season generously. Drizzle with olive oil, then close the parcels and roast over the fire until the garlic and onion are tender.

*Braaied Green Tomatoes and Rosemary-smoked Chicken (page 75)*

*Grilled Pepper Baskets*

# Mediterranean Cabbage Slices
Serves 4

1 large cabbage, sliced into four thick rounds
olive oil
coarse salt and freshly ground black pepper
1–2 garlic cloves, crushed
tomato pasta sauce

mozzarella cheese, grated
a handful of black olives, pitted and sliced
a generous sprinkling of Italian herbs

1 Place each cabbage round onto a piece of buttered foil large enough to enclose the sides of the cabbage. Drizzle generously with the olive oil, then season.
2 Combine the garlic and tomato sauce. Spread the tomato sauce over each cabbage slice and top with the cheese and olives. Sprinkle with the herbs and roast over the coals until the cabbage is tender and the cheese melted.


# Grilled Pepper Baskets
Serves 6

200 g feta cheese, cubed
100 g black olives, drained, halved and pitted
50 g sun-dried tomatoes in oil, drained and
  chopped
1–2 cloves garlic, crushed

45 ml fresh origanum, chopped
25 ml olive oil
salt and freshly ground black pepper
3 large red or yellow peppers, halved lengthwise
  and seeded

1 Combine all the ingredients except the peppers in a bowl and season well. Divide the mixture among the pepper halves and fill each half.
2 Cook over a medium heat until the peppers are slightly charred and the cheese is starting to melt. Serve immediately.


# Avocado and Bacon Wraps
Serves 8

375 ml grated cheddar cheese
8 rashers bacon, chopped and fried until crispy
  (omit the bacon for a vegetarian option)
2 ripe avocados, diced

2 small tomatoes, finely diced
a few sprigs fresh coriander, chopped
salt and freshly ground black pepper to taste
8 small flour tortillas

1 Mix the cheese with the bacon, avocados, tomatoes and coriander. Season with salt and pepper.
2 Spoon some of the mixture in a line along one side of each tortilla and roll up carefully. Position two wraps, side by side, in the centre of a large square of heavy-duty foil. Fold up the sides to form a sealed parcel. Repeat with the remaining tortillas.
3 Place the parcels on the side of a medium-hot braai and cook for 10 minutes, turning, until they are heated through and the cheese has melted. Unwrap and serve immediately.

# Baked Sweet Potatoes with Savoury Butter
Serves 8

8 medium sweet potatoes

**SAVOURY BUTTER**

30 ml chopped fresh flat-leaf parsley

10 ml garlic, roughly chopped

4 sun-dried tomatoes, drained

2 red chillies, deseeded and roughly chopped

10 ml chopped fresh rosemary leaves

15 ml lemon juice

2 ml chilli powder

250 g butter, softened

salt to taste

1  Combine all the ingredients for the savoury butter, except the butter, in a food processor. Process until finely chopped, then season with a little salt. Add the butter and pulse until well mixed.
2  Spoon onto a piece of clingfilm, then shape into a log about 3 cm in diameter. Wrap and chill until required.
3  Scrub the sweet potatoes, prick all over with a fork and wrap each in a double layer of lightly oiled foil. Place in the coals of the braai and cook for 30–45 minutes, turning regularly, or until tender when tested with a skewer.
4  Carefully peel away the foil, cut a line in the top of each sweet potato and press on the sides to open it up. Top each one with a slice of savoury butter.


# Ratatouille
Serves 4

100 ml olive oil

2 red onions, sliced

10 ml crushed garlic

1 medium brinjal, sliced

1 green pepper, seeded and cut into strips

1 red pepper, seeded and cut into strips

4 small baby marrows, washed and sliced

2 tomatoes, seeded and quartered

15 ml chopped fresh basil

salt and freshly ground black pepper

30 ml chopped fresh parsley

1  Place a large pan on the kettle braai. Add the oil and, when it is hot, add the onions and garlic and cook for about 5 minutes, stirring until the onion is soft. Add the brinjal, peppers and baby marrows.
2  Cook for a further 5 minutes, stirring frequently. Stir in the tomatoes, basil and seasoning, and sprinkle with the parsley.
3  Place the lid on the braai and cook for about 20–30 minutes. Serve hot or cold as a main dish or with chicken, lamb, fish or beef.

*Baked Sweet Potatoes with Savoury Butter*

*Pumpkin and Feta Bake*

# Butternut and Potato Bake
Serves 8

1 butternut, peeled, seeded and sliced into
   5 mm-thick pieces
4 large potatoes, peeled and sliced into
   5 mm-thick pieces

1 x 40 g packet white onion soup
250 ml cream
250 ml milk

1  Layer the butternut and potato slices in a buttered ovenproof dish and sprinkle onion soup over
   the top.
2  Pour over the cream and milk and bake at 160 °C for about 60 minutes or until the vegetables
   are tender.


# Pumpkin and Feta Bake
Serves 8

2 kg pumpkin or butternut, cut into long slices
   and cooked until just tender
200 g feta cheese, drained and crumbled
60 g butter

salt and freshly ground black pepper to taste
100 g Parmesan cheese, grated
125 ml breadcrumbs
45 ml olive oil

1  Drain the pumpkin or butternut and remove the skin if desired.
2  Arrange the slices in a buttered ovenproof dish, then sprinkle over the feta. Dot with the butter
   and season with salt and pepper.
3  Mix the Parmesan and breadcrumbs and sprinkle over the dish. Drizzle with the olive oil. Bake at
   200° C for 20–30 minutes until golden brown.


# Grilled Baby Marrows and Brinjals
Serves 4

300 g baby marrows, sliced lengthwise into
   3 mm slices
300 g brinjals, sliced lengthwise into 3 mm slices
olive oil

45 ml chopped fresh parsley
45 ml crushed garlic
salt and freshly ground black pepper

1  Place the marrows and brinjals in a colander and sprinkle with salt. Leave to stand for
   30 minutes to allow the excess liquid to drain from the vegetables.
2  Grill on the braai for a few minutes on both sides. Dress with the olive oil, parsley, garlic and
   seasoning.

# Veggie Burger
Makes 6

250 ml red lentils

30 ml oil

1 large onion, finely chopped

15 ml curry powder

15 ml chopped fresh ginger

1 x 425 g can chickpeas, drained

1 egg

2 baby marrows, grated

60 ml chopped fresh parsley

30 ml chopped fresh coriander

500 ml fresh breadcrumbs

salt and freshly ground black pepper to taste

flour for dusting

olive oil for brushing

**TO SERVE**

wholewheat rolls

1 onion, cut into rings and fried

1 punnet baby tomatoes, lightly fried

baby marrows, cut into thin ribbons with a potato
     peeler and sautéed

1   Place the lentils in a saucepan, cover with water and bring to the boil. Simmer for 10–15 minutes or until tender. Drain well.
2   Heat the oil in a frying pan and cook the onion until softened. Add the curry powder and ginger, and cook for 1 minute. Remove and cool.
3   Combine the chickpeas, half the lentils, the onion mixture and the egg in a food processor and blend until smooth.
4   Transfer to a bowl, then mix in the baby marrows, the remaining lentils, parsley, coriander and breadcrumbs. Mix until well blended and season well.
5   Using wet hands, divide the mixture into 6 burgers. Dust with the flour and refrigerate for at least 1 hour before cooking.
6   Brush with the olive oil and cook on a heated braai griddle for 5 minutes on each side. Serve on lightly buttered rolls topped with the fried onion rings, baby tomatoes and baby marrows.

# Roast Potato Wedges with Honey and Olive Oil
Serves 6–8

6–8 large potatoes, peeled and cut into wedges

60 ml olive oil

30 ml whole grain mustard

45 ml runny honey

salt and freshly ground black pepper

1   Place the wedges in a saucepan, cover with cold water and bring to the boil. Cook until just tender. Drain well.
2   Whisk together the oil, mustard, honey, salt and pepper.
3   Place the potatoes in a roasting pan, drizzle over the oil mixture and toss until evenly coated.
4   Bake at 190 °C for 40–50 minutes or until golden and cooked through.

*Veggie Burger*

# Breads

# Boma Pot Bread
Makes 1 loaf

750 ml self-raising flour
5 ml salt
1 x 340 ml can beer

60 ml sunflower seeds
1 x 410 g can sweetcorn kernels
15 ml chopped fresh parsley

1   Mix together all the ingredients except the parsley in a large mixing bowl and knead well. Place the dough in a greased cast-iron pot, cover and leave to stand for 1 hour.
2   Just before baking, sprinkle with the chopped parsley and bake over hot coals for about 45 minutes.


# Feta, Onion and Potato Bread
Makes 1 small round loaf

300 ml self-raising flour, plus a little extra for the
   top of the loaf
5 ml salt
3 ml cayenne pepper
5 ml mustard powder
1 large potato, peeled

1 bunch spring onions, finely sliced
15 ml chopped fresh thyme
125 g feta cheese, cubed
1 extra large egg
60 ml milk
5 ml whole grain mustard

1   Sift the flour, salt, cayenne pepper and mustard powder into a large mixing bowl.
2   Grate the potato into the flour mixture. Add the spring onions, thyme and the feta. Blend with a palette knife.
3   Beat the egg with the milk and mustard, then pour over the flour mixture and bring together to form a loose, rough dough.
4   Transfer to a baking sheet sprayed with non-stick cooking spray and pat into a 15 cm round. Bake on the baking sheet over an indirect fire or gas fire for 45 minutes. Best served warm with lots of butter.


# Garlic, Potato and Rosemary Pot Bread
Makes 1 loaf

1 egg
100 ml cream
10 ml crushed garlic
200 g potatoes, cooked and mashed

750 ml self-raising flour
10 ml salt
30 ml fresh rosemary, chopped

1   Whisk together the egg, cream and garlic. Mix this into the mashed potatoes and gradually add the flour, salt and rosemary. Turn the mixture out onto a lightly floured surface, knead lightly and shape into a round.
2   Place in an oiled cast-iron casserole. Mark the top with wedge lines.
3   Cook over an indirect fire in the centre of the grid. Cover with the kettle braai lid and bake for 30–35 minutes. Serve with lots of butter.

*Boma Pot Bread (back) and Feta, Onion and Potato Bread*

*Tomato and Olive Loaf*

## Tomato and Olive Loaf
Makes 1 loaf

4 extra large eggs
500 ml self-raising flour
5 ml baking powder
45 ml olive oil
30 ml tomato purée
100 g black olives, stoned, dried and chopped

8 sun-dried tomatoes in olive oil, roughly chopped
a generous handful fresh basil, chopped
5 ml salt
a good grinding of black pepper
coarse salt for sprinkling

1  In a large bowl, beat the eggs. Sift in the flour and baking powder, and mix with a wooden spoon.
2  Add the olive oil and tomato purée. Knead lightly until well combined. Add the remaining ingredients except the coarse salt and knead gently. Press into a 23 x 13 cm greased loaf pan.
3  Sprinkle lightly with the coarse salt. Bake for 45 minutes over an indirect heat, in a gas braai or in the oven at 190 °C.


## Mediterranean Bread-and-butter Pudding
Serves 4–6

30 ml butter, softened
60 ml sun-dried tomato pesto
1 French loaf
150 g mozzarella cheese, thinly sliced
2–3 large ripe tomatoes, sliced
300 ml milk

200 ml cream
3 extra large eggs
15 ml chopped fresh origanum
salt and freshly ground black pepper
50 g Parmesan cheese, grated

1  Blend together the butter and pesto in a bowl.
2  Slice the French loaf and spread one side of each slice with the pesto mixture. In a rectangular foil container, layer the bread slices with the mozzarella and tomatoes, overlapping each new layer with the next.
3  Beat together the milk, cream, eggs and origanum. Season well and pour over the bread. Leave to stand for 5 minutes.
4  Sprinkle over the Parmesan and bake the 'pudding' over an indirect or gas fire for 40–60 minutes or until golden brown and just set. Serve immediately.

# French Cheese Tart

Makes 1 large tart

| DOUGH | FILLING |
|---|---|
| 750 ml cake flour | 125 g Cheddar cheese, thinly sliced |
| 10 ml salt | 125 g Edam cheese, thinly sliced |
| 1 x 10 g sachet instant dry yeast | 125 ml sour cream |
| 125 ml milk, warmed | 1 extra large egg |
| 2 extra large eggs | 1 extra large egg yolk |
| 60 g butter, softened | salt and freshly ground black pepper |
| | ground nutmeg |

1   Prepare the dough by sifting the flour and salt into a large bowl. Add the yeast and stir through.
2   Combine the milk with the eggs and butter, and add to the flour mixture. Combine until a soft dough is formed, then knead on a lightly floured surface for 5 minutes. Cover and leave to rise in a warm place for approximately 45 minutes until doubled in size.
3   Knock back the dough and roll into a 30 cm round. Press into a pizza pan or baking tray.
4   For the filling, arrange the cheese in an even layer over the base of the tart.
5   Beat together the cream, egg, egg yolk, salt and plenty of black pepper and nutmeg. Pour this mixture over the dough. Cover and leave to rise for about 15 minutes until puffy.
6   Bake over indirect heat or in a gas braai for 40–50 minutes until the filling is set and the crust is golden brown.


# Biltong Bread Rolls

Makes 24 rolls

| | FILLING |
|---|---|
| 5 x 250 ml cake flour | |
| 10 ml salt | 125 g butter, softened |
| 15 ml sugar | 3 garlic cloves, crushed |
| 1 x 10 g packet instant dry yeast | 60 ml chopped fresh parsley |
| 25 ml olive oil | 250 ml grated biltong |
| 250–300 ml lukewarm water to mix | |
| beaten egg, to glaze | |

1   Combine the dry ingredients in a mixing bowl. Add the oil and enough water to form a dough that is soft but not sticky. Knead well until smooth and elastic. Place into an oiled plastic bag and leave to rise for approximately 45 minutes until doubled in size.
2   Knock down the dough, then divide into ping-pong-sized balls. Cover and rest for 5 minutes.
3   Prepare the filling by combining all the ingredients and mixing well. Roll each ball of dough into an 8–10 cm disc, spread with some of the filling and roll up like a pancake.
4   Place seam side down into a greased roasting pan. Repeat with the remaining balls. Using a small, sharp knife, cut a slit in the top of each roll to expose the filling. Cover and leave to rise for 20 minutes.
5   Brush with the beaten egg and bake at 200 °C for 30 minutes until golden brown. Remove and serve warm.

*French Cheese Tart (back) and Biltong Bread Rolls*

*Rustic Rosemary Flat Bread*

# Rustic Rosemary Flatbread

Makes 8

500 ml flour

5 ml instant dry yeast

10 ml salt

10 ml olive oil, plus extra for brushing

250 ml soda water

fresh rosemary, finely chopped

coarse sea salt and freshly ground black pepper

1   Combine the flour, yeast and salt in a large mixing bowl. Add the oil and enough soda water to make a dough that is soft but not sticky. Knead for 5 minutes until smooth.

2   Divide the dough into eight pieces and roll out into rough rounds about 15 cm in diameter. Place on a baking sheet lightly sprinkled with flour, cover with a damp cloth and leave to stand for 5 minutes. Brush with olive oil and sprinkle with the rosemary, coarse salt and pepper.

3   Place a lightly oiled baking tray onto the kettle braai grid and heat for 5 minutes. Place four breads at a time onto the heated tray, close the lid and bake for 5–7 minutes, turning halfway through the baking time.

NOTE: When cooking this type of bread, the fire should not be too large or too hot.

# Cracked Pepper and Cranberry Bread

Makes 1 large or 2 small loaves

4 x 250 ml cake flour

10 ml freshly ground black pepper

10 ml salt

1 x 10 g sachet instant dry yeast

30 ml olive oil

±400 ml warm water

200 g dried cranberries

100 g pecan nuts, chopped

1   Combine the flour, pepper, salt and yeast in a large mixing bowl. Stir in the olive oil and enough warm water to form a soft but not sticky dough. Turn out onto a lightly floured work surface and knead for about 5 minutes until the dough is smooth and elastic.

2   Place in an oiled plastic bag and leave in a warm place for approximately 45 minutes until doubled in size. Knock down the dough, then incorporate the cranberries and nuts. Don't over work the dough at this point.

3   Shape the dough roughly into a round and place on a greased baking sheet. Using scissors, slash the top of the loaf and sprinkle with a little flour. Cover and leave to rise again for about 20 minutes.

4   Bake at 200 °C for 45–50 minutes until the bread sounds hollow when tapped underneath. Place on a cooling rack to cool completely. Serve with lots of butter and mature cheese.

# Olive Oil Bread

Makes 1 large flat bread

750 ml bread flour

1 x 10 g sachet instant dry yeast

5 ml salt

10 ml sugar

60 ml olive oil

250–300 ml warm water

**TOPPING**

100 ml olive oil

a strip lemon rind

25 ml chopped fresh thyme leaves

5–10 ml coarse salt, plus extra for sprinkling

1  Sift the flour into a mixing bowl. Add the yeast, salt and sugar. Add the oil and enough warm water to form a soft but not sticky dough. Knead well until smooth and elastic.

2  Place in an oiled plastic bag and leave in a warm place for approximately 45 minutes until doubled in size. Turn the dough out onto a floured surface and knead lightly. Grease a 20 x 30 cm swiss roll pan and roll out the dough to fit into the pan. Cover with oiled clingfilm and leave until well risen.

3  For the topping, combine all the ingredients and leave to marinate while preparing the dough. When the dough has risen, make indentations in it. Remove the rind from the flavoured oil and drizzle the oil over the dough.

4  Bake in the oven at 200 °C for 20–30 minutes or until golden brown. Place on a cooling rack and sprinkle over the coarse salt.

# Spinach, Feta and Olive Damper

Makes 1 loaf

750 ml self-raising flour

5 ml salt

10 ml freshly ground black pepper

15 ml sugar

50 g butter

200 g feta cheese, cubed or roughly crumbled

200 g baby spinach leaves, finely chopped

100 g black olives, pitted and chopped

125 ml buttermilk

± 250 ml water

1  Combine the flour, salt, pepper and sugar in a bowl. Rub in the butter. Stir in the cheese, spinach, olives, buttermilk (reserve a little for brushing) and enough water to form a stiff dough.

2  Divide the dough into two, shape into 10 cm rounds and place onto a greased baking tray. Cut a cross 1 cm deep into the rounds and brush the tops with the reserved buttermilk. Bake at 180 °C for 40–50 minutes until cooked. Serve warm with butter.

# Fruit and Nut Health Bread

Makes 2 loaves

4 x 250 ml wholewheat flour

500 ml digestive bran

125 ml sesame seeds

125 ml poppy seeds

125 ml sunflower seeds

125 ml raisins

125 ml pecan nuts, chopped

125 ml dried apricots, chopped

30 ml bicarbonate of soda

1 litre Greek yoghurt

125 ml honey

1  Combine all the dry ingredients in a large bowl and mix well.

2  Mix together the yoghurt and honey, add to the dry ingredients and mix until a stiff batter is formed.

3  Spoon into two 23 x 13 cm greased, base-lined loaf pans and bake at 180 °C for 40–50 minutes or until a skewer inserted comes out clean. Remove from the pans and cool.

# Cheese and Onion Quick Bread

Makes 4 mini loaves

500 ml self-raising flour

2 ml salt

freshly ground black pepper

2 red onions, finely chopped

100 ml chopped fresh parsley

100 ml chopped chives

60 ml grated Cheddar cheese

250 g cream cheese

1 extra large egg

15 ml whole grain mustard

150–180 ml milk

1  Combine the flour, salt, pepper, half of the onions, half of the herbs and the Cheddar cheese in a bowl.

2  Combine the cream cheese, egg and mustard, and stir into the dry ingredients with enough milk to form a soft but not sticky dough. Turn out onto a floured surface and divide into four.

3  Shape into four oval-shaped mini loaves and coat each loaf with the remaining chopped onions and herbs.

4  Place on a greased baking sheet and bake at 180 °C for 25–30 minutes, or until a skewer comes out clean.

# Salads

# Grilled Baby Marrows with Feta and Pine Nuts

Serves 4

500 g baby marrows

olive oil for brushing

DRESSING

50 ml lemon juice

45 ml olive oil

2 cloves garlic, crushed

60–80 ml chopped fresh mint

salt and freshly ground black pepper

100 g feta cheese, crumbled

50 g pine nuts, toasted

1  Slice the baby marrows lengthwise into long slices about 2 mm thick (a mandolin will make this task much easier).
2  Brush the slices with olive oil and arrange as many slices as will fit onto a vegetable grate on the braai and cook until slightly charred on both sides. Remove and set aside.
3  Combine all the dressing ingredients except the feta and pine nuts, and mix well – a screw-top jar works well for this. Arrange the cooked baby marrows on a platter and pour over the dressing. Sprinkle with feta and pine nuts.

# Lebanese Potato Salad

*This is a healthy version of potato salad*

Serves 6

6–8 potatoes

125 ml olive oil

60–80 ml lemon juice

3 cloves garlic, chopped

plenty of salt and freshly ground black pepper

60 ml chopped fresh Italian parsley

1  Boil the potatoes until tender. Drain and cool until you can handle them, but they should not be cold.
2  Peel the potatoes and cut into 2–3 cm cubes.
3  Combine the oil, lemon juice and garlic, and pour over the potatoes while still warm. Season well with salt and pepper and mix in the parsley. This salad is even more delicious the next day.

# Sweetcorn and Fresh Herb Salad

Serves 4

4 cobs of fresh sweetcorn

1 red onion, finely chopped

125 ml finely chopped fresh coriander

80 ml finely chopped fresh mint

100 ml lime or lemon juice

50 ml sweet chilli sauce

30 ml fish sauce

15 ml honey

1  Cut the sweetcorn from the cobs with a sharp knife and place in a bowl. Add the chopped onion and herbs, and mix well.
2  Mix together the lime or lemon juice, sweet chilli sauce, fish sauce and honey. Pour over the sweetcorn mixture and mix well. Serve immediately.

*Sweetcorn and Fresh Herb Salad and Espatada (page 26)*

*Chickpea Salad and Chilli Chicken Thighs (page 67)*

# Chickpea Salad

Serves 4

2 x 400 g cans chickpeas, rinsed and drained

250 g cherry tomatoes

1 cucumber, seeded and diced

1 red onion, halved and sliced

60 ml chopped fresh mint

30 ml chopped fresh coriander

50 ml lemon juice

50 ml olive oil

5 ml prepared mustard

10 ml runny honey

1 clove garlic, chopped

1 red chilli, seeded and chopped

1   Place the chickpeas, cherry tomatoes (if the tomatoes are large, halve them), cucumber and onion into a bowl.

2   Combine the remaining ingredients and mix well. Pour over the chickpeas and mix well. The flavour improves on standing.


# Pasta Rice Salad

Serves 4–6

125 g pasta rice

125 g small rosa tomatoes

½ English cucumber, seeded and diced

125 g mozzarella cheese, cut into small cubes

1 bunch spring onions, finely chopped

100 g black olives, halved and pitted

125 ml fresh basil leaves, chopped

**DRESSING**

80 ml olive oil

45 ml lemon juice

1 clove garlic, crushed

salt and freshly ground black pepper

1   Cook the pasta rice according to the instructions; watch carefully as it can overcook very quickly. Drain immediately and rinse well under cold water. Place in a bowl with the remaining ingredients.

2   Mix the ingredients for the dressing well and pour over the pasta mixture. Mix well and serve.


# Oriental Cabbage Salad

Serves 4–6

½ cabbage, finely shredded

100 g slivered almonds, toasted

100 g sunflower seeds, toasted

1 packet one-minute noodles, broken up

**DRESSING**

125 ml sunflower oil

80 ml wine vinegar

100 ml sugar

15 ml soy sauce

1   Combine the cabbage, nuts and seeds in a large bowl. Combine all the dressing ingredients, mix thoroughly, pour over the cabbage and toss well. Leave the salad to stand for 30 minutes so the flavours can mingle.

2   Fry the noodles in a dry, non-stick pan until just golden. Remove and cool. Sprinkle the crumbled noodles over the salad just before serving.

# Haloumi Salad
Serves 6

200 g Haloumi cheese, drained, cut into slices
seasoned flour
olive oil for frying
2 red onions, sliced
1 pillow packet salad greens
pita bread, cut into triangles

DRESSING
30 ml lime juice
60 ml capers, rinsed, drained and chopped
120 ml olive oil
15 ml runny honey
5 ml whole grain mustard
5 ml crushed garlic
salt and freshly ground black pepper

1   Pat the cheese dry with kitchen paper and toss in the seasoned flour.
2   Heat a little olive oil in a frying pan and fry the cheese until golden brown on both sides. Remove from the heat and drain well on paper towel.
3   Fry the sliced onions until crisp. Place the lettuce onto a serving platter and arrange the cheese on top.
4   For the dressing, mix together the lime juice, capers, olive oil, honey, mustard and garlic with seasoning and mix well to make the dressing.
5   Pour the dressing over the salad and top with the onions and pita bread. Serve immediately.


# Pasta Salad with Herb Dressing
Serves 6

250 g short pasta
olive oil
100 ml fresh parsley
100 ml fresh basil leaves
1 clove garlic, crushed
1 bunch spring onions, chopped
125 ml thick mayonnaise

125 ml plain yoghurt
60 ml olive oil
salt and freshly ground black pepper to taste
pinch of sugar
125 ml black olives, pitted
125 g feta cheese, crumbled

1   Cook the pasta in salted boiling water until *al dente*. Drain and rinse.
2   Toss in a dash of olive oil and cool.
3   Place the parsley, basil, garlic, spring onions, mayonnaise, yoghurt and oil into a blender, and blend until smooth. Season to taste and add the pinch of sugar.
4   Stir the dressing into the pasta to coat evenly. Toss in the olives and feta and serve.

*Haloumi Salad and Rosemary-smoked Chicken (page 75)*

*Crunch Salad with Honey Mustard Dressing and Chicken Satay (page 71)*

# Strawberry and Asparagus Salad with Parmesan Crisps
Serves 4

1 bunch fresh green asparagus
olive oil
salt and freshly ground black pepper
1 pillow packet rocket, washed
balsamic vinegar, plus 80 ml extra for
  the reduction

30 ml honey
250 g strawberries

**PARMESAN CRISPS**
250 ml freshly grated Parmesan cheese

1  Coat the asparagus with a little olive oil and cook on a hot grill pan until tender. Season with salt and pepper. Toss the rocket leaves lightly in a little olive oil and balsamic vinegar, just to moisten them.
2  To make the balsamic reduction, combine 80 ml balsamic vinegar and honey in a small saucepan over low heat. Bring to the boil, reduce the heat and simmer gently until the mixture reduces and thickens slightly.
3  To make the Parmesan crisps, place 4 mounds of about 60 ml Parmesan onto a baking tray lined with baking paper, spaced well apart, and place in the oven at 180 °C for 5–8 minutes until melted and golden brown. Remove from the oven and cool.
4  Arrange the asparagus, rocket and strawberries on serving plates and place Parmesan crisps on top. Drizzle with the balsamic reduction. Serve immediately.


# Crunch Salad with Honey Mustard Dressing
Serves 4

2 baby cabbages, finely sliced
2 sticks celery, sliced
3 spring onions, chopped
6 radishes, thinly sliced
50 g pecan nuts
1 red-skinned apple, cored and thinly sliced
1 green-skinned apple, cored and thinly sliced
250 ml croutons

**DRESSING**
30 ml whole grain mustard
15 ml honey
90 ml olive oil
30 ml white wine vinegar
salt and freshly ground black pepper

1  Combine the cabbage, celery, spring onions, radishes, nuts and apples in a large bowl, then add the croutons.
2  For the dressing, combine all the ingredients in a jar and shake well.
3  Spoon the dressing over the salad and toss to combine.

# Carrot and Baby Marrow Salad
Serves 6

500 ml coarsely grated carrots
500 ml coarsely grated baby marrows
1 bunch spring onions, finely chopped
45 ml light soy sauce
45 ml sweet chilli sauce

15 ml sesame oil
2 cm piece of ginger, peeled and grated
large handful of fresh coriander, finely chopped
100 ml peanuts, toasted and crushed

1  Combine the carrot, baby marrow and spring onions in a large mixing bowl. Combine the soy sauce, chilli sauce, sesame oil, ginger and coriander.
2  Pour over the salad, sprinkle with the peanuts and toss gently. Leave to stand for one hour before serving.


# Grilled Pear, Asparagus and Rocket Salad
Serves 4

4 pears
50 ml olive oil
25 ml lemon juice
1 bunch asparagus

1 packet rocket, washed
50 g toasted pine nuts
Parmesan shavings
store-bought balsamic glaze

1  Cut the pears into quarters and brush with a mixture of the olive oil and lemon juice.
2  Wash and trim the asparagus and also brush with the olive oil and lemon juice. Cook the asparagus and pears over a high heat on a vegetable griddle until just tender. Remove and set aside. Cut each asparagus spear into three.
3  Arrange the rocket on a serving platter, top with the asparagus and pears, sprinkle with pine nuts and Parmesan shavings, and drizzle with balsamic glaze.


# A Truly South African Salad
Serves 6

6 naartjies, peeled and sliced horizontally into 3
2 bulbs fennel, thinly sliced
3 large sticks celery, thinly sliced
1 bunch spring onions, finely sliced

80 ml macadamia nut oil
salt and freshly ground black pepper
80 g thinly sliced biltong
50 ml chopped toasted macadamia nuts

1  Arrange the naartjie slices in a single layer on a large platter. Combine the fennel, celery, spring onions and macadamia nut oil, and mix well.
2  Scatter over the naartjie slices and season with salt and pepper. Drizzle over a little extra oil and garnish with slices of biltong and macadamia nuts.

*A Truly South African Salad with Venison and Apricot Kebabs (page 50)*

*Grapefruit, Avocado and Prawn Salad and Calamari Tubes with Lemon and Chilli (page 85)*

# Roasted Butternut and Chickpea Salad

Serves 6

1 large butternut, peeled and cubed

45 ml olive oil

generous pinch of dried chilli flakes

salt and freshly ground black pepper

1 x 400 g can chickpeas, drained

45 ml fresh coriander, finely chopped

1 pillow packet of rocket or baby spinach

**DRESSING**

6 pieces sun-dried tomato in olive oil

45 ml red wine vinegar

3 cloves garlic

15 ml balsamic vinegar

100 ml olive oil

5–10 ml sugar

salt and freshly ground black pepper

1   Preheat the oven to 190° C. Spread out the butternut on a baking sheet.
2   Combine the olive oil, chilli flakes and seasoning. Pour over the butternut and toss to coat. Roast until the butternut is tender and just turning brown. This will take about 40 minutes.
3   For the dressing, place all the ingredients in a food processor. Process until smooth, adding more olive oil if too thick.
4   Heat the chickpeas in a small pan and pour over the dressing while still warm. Combine the chickpeas with the pumpkin. Fold in the fresh coriander and season.
5   Serve on a bed of rocket or spinach. Best enjoyed at room temperature.

# Grapefruit, Avocado and Prawn Salad

Serves 4

1 small red onion, thinly sliced

1 grapefruit, peeled and segmented

1 bunch spring onions, thinly sliced

60 ml chopped fresh mint leaves

60 ml chopped fresh coriander

1 red chilli, seeded and thinly sliced

60 ml roasted unsalted peanuts, roughly chopped

25 ml coconut shavings, toasted

**DRESSING**

1 clove garlic, crushed

10 ml palm sugar or honey

30 ml lime juice

15 ml fish sauce

15 ml sweet chilli sauce

300 g prawns, tails on, cooked

2 avocados, peeled and sliced

1   Arrange the onion, grapefruit, spring onions, mint and coriander on a serving plate. Sprinkle with the chilli, peanuts and coconut.
2   For the dressing, combine the garlic, palm sugar or honey, lime juice, fish sauce and sweet chilli sauce, and mix well.
3   Arrange the prawns and avocado slices on top of the salad. Pour over the dressing just before serving.

# Hummus, Carrot and Sesame Salad

Serves 6

2 x 400 g can chickpeas, drained

100 ml olive oil

2 cloves garlic, crushed

15 ml ground cumin

juice of 1 lemon

pinch of chilli powder

salt and freshly ground black pepper

4 large carrots, peeled and finely grated

small handful of raisins

30 ml sesame seeds, toasted

pillow packet of baby spinach and rocket leaves

splash of extra olive oil

splash of balsamic vinegar

20 ml tahini

1   Combine the drained chickpeas, olive oil and garlic in a food processor or blender, and process until smooth. Add the cumin, lemon juice and chilli powder. Process again.
2   Season generously and set aside. Combine the carrots, raisins and sesame seeds.
3   Scatter a handful of green leaves on individual serving plates. Top with the carrot mixture and spoon over the chickpea mixture.
4   Just before serving, combine the extra olive oil, balsamic vinegar and tahini. Pour over each salad and serve.

# Gado Gado Salad

*Indonesian in origin, the ingredients can be varied but this salad is always served with a peanut sauce*

Serves 4

1 medium-sized cabbage, shredded

200 g green beans, topped and tailed

2 large firm red tomatoes, each cut into eight wedges

1 small cauliflower, broken into florets

½ small English cucumber, cut into chunks

1 small pineapple, peeled and cut into chunks

4 hard-boiled eggs, quartered

**PEANUT SAUCE**

180 ml crunchy peanut butter

60 ml water

30 ml light soya sauce

30 ml sweet chilli sauce

125 ml coconut milk

1   Lightly blanch the cabbage and beans separately, until just tender but still crisp. Drain and rinse under cold water.
2   Arrange the cabbage, beans, tomatoes, cauliflower, cucumber, pineapple and eggs on a large platter.
3   For the sauce, combine all the ingredients in a small pan and heat over a low heat, stirring until the sauce is smooth. Serve the salad accompanied by the peanut sauce.

# Ginger Noodle Salad

Serves 4

250 g Oriental noodles, soaked in boiling water and
  drained
50 ml peanut oil
1 clove garlic, crushed
1 red chilli, seeded and sliced
6 pieces stem ginger in syrup, drained and finely
  chopped, retaining 30 ml syrup

juice of 1 lime
60 ml sweet soy sauce (ketjap manis)
large handful fresh coriander, chopped
1 bunch chives, finely sliced
handful toasted peanuts, crushed

1  Place the drained noodles in a serving dish.
2  Combine the oil, garlic, chilli, chopped ginger and syrup, lime juice and sweet soy sauce in a screw-top jar.
3  Toss the coriander and chives into the noodles. Shake the dressing ingredients and pour over the noodles. Toss to mix through. Sprinkle over nuts.

# Avocado, Prawn and Papino Salad

Serves 6

1 large butter lettuce
2 avocados, peeled, pitted and sliced
2 small papinos, peeled, pitted and sliced
300–500 g prawns, cooked

**DRESSING**
80 ml papino pips
50 ml brown sugar
50 ml olive oil
100 ml white wine vinegar

1  Arrange the lettuce, avocados and papinos onto a salad platter, then scatter over the prawns.
2  To make the dressing, place the pips into a mini chopper or blender, and blend until roughly chopped. Add the sugar, oil and vinegar, and blend until well mixed. Pour over the salad just before serving.

# Desserts

# White Chocolate and Amarula Cheesecake
Serves 8–10

1 packet Marie biscuits, crushed

90 g butter, melted

500 g thick cream cheese

1 x 397 g can condensed milk

200 g white chocolate, melted and cooled

15 ml gelatine, softened in 50 ml cold water

250 ml cream, whipped

80 ml Amarula Cream liqueur

**TOPPING**

250 g dark chocolate

100 ml Amarula Cream liqueur

1   Combine the biscuits and butter and press into a 23 cm springform tin. Place in the fridge to harden.
2   Combine the cream cheese and condensed milk, then beat in the melted chocolate.
3   Melt the gelatine in the microwave for 10 seconds and beat into the cheese mixture. Fold in the whipped cream and liqueur.
4   Pour the mixture into the prepared biscuit base and place in the fridge to set for 3–4 hours. Melt the chocolate and liqueur for the topping and mix until smooth.
5   Spoon the topping over the cheesecake before serving.


# Apple Roly-poly
Serves 6

500 ml cake flour

15 ml baking powder

125 g butter

180 ml milk

4 apples, peeled and grated

50 ml sugar

5 ml cinnamon

**SAUCE**

375 ml sugar

250 ml water

100 g butter

3 ml ground cinnamon

1   Sift the flour and baking powder. Rub in the butter. Add enough milk to make a stiff dough, mixing lightly. Place the dough onto a floured surface and roll out into a large rectangle measuring approximately 30 x 22 cm.
2   Mix together the apples, sugar and cinnamon and spread onto the dough. Roll up as for a swiss roll, then cut into slices and place cut side up into a greased ovenproof dish.
3   To prepare the sauce, place all the ingredients in a saucepan and bring to the boil. Pour over the slices.
4   Bake at 180 °C for 30–40 minutes until cooked. Serve warm with custard or cream.

*White Chocolate and Amarula Cheesecake*

*Camembert Fondue*

# Caramel Apple Tart

Serves 4–6

2 eggs
180 ml sugar
60 ml milk
30 g butter
250 ml self-raising flour
1 x 410 g can pie apples
15 ml lemon juice
25 ml castor sugar

**SAUCE**
250 ml cream
150 ml sugar
60 g butter
5 ml caramel essence

1  Beat the eggs and sugar until pale and thick.
2  Heat the milk and butter, then cool slightly. Add to the egg mixture, then beat in the flour. Mix the apples with the lemon juice and castor sugar, and place in the bottom of a deep, greased 20 cm ovenproof dish. Pour the batter over the apple mixture.
3  Bake at 180 °C for 30–40 minutes until cooked. A skewer inserted in the centre should come out clean. Remove from the oven and pour over the sauce.
4  To make the sauce, boil together all the ingredients.

# Strawberry Ice Cream

Serves 8–10

600 g strawberries, cleaned and hulled
200 ml castor sugar
30 ml Kirsch or berry liqueur

150 ml orange juice
100 ml lemon juice
250 ml cream, whipped

1  Place the strawberries, castor sugar, liqueur and juices into a blender and blend until smooth. Mix in the whipped cream.
2  Pour into a container and freeze until required. Remove 20 minutes before serving to soften slightly.

# Camembert Fondue

*This is great for either a starter or as a dessert served with fresh fruit*
Serves 8–10

1 large ripe Camembert cheese
grated rind of 1 orange
1 large sprig fresh rosemary, finely chopped
1 clove garlic, finely chopped

freshly ground black pepper
45 ml olive oil
45 ml white wine

1  Remove the paper from the cheese and place on a large piece of heavy-duty foil.
2  Make a few holes in the top of the cheese and sprinkle over the orange rind, rosemary and garlic. Grind over some pepper, pour over the oil and wine, and seal the foil tightly.
3  Place on a baking tray in the oven at 180 °C for 15–20 minutes until the cheese is nice and soft. Serve with chunks of French loaf for dipping, and seasonal fresh fruit.

# Honey and Nougat Semi-fredo
Serves 4

2 eggs, separated
60 ml honey
150 ml icing sugar

500 ml cream, whipped
150 g soft nougat, chopped
50 g blanched almonds, roasted and chopped

1 Combine the egg yolks, honey and 60 ml of the icing sugar in the bowl of an electric mixer, and beat until pale and thick. Set aside.
2 Place the egg whites into another bowl and beat until soft peaks form. Gradually add the remaining icing sugar and beat until glossy. Add this to the egg yolk mixture, mix well, then fold in the whipped cream, nougat and almonds.
3 Spoon the mixture into a lined 20 cm springform tin and freeze for 3–4 hours. Soften in the fridge before cutting into slices.


# Rolled Pavlova
Serves 8–10

6 extra-large egg whites
5 ml vinegar
375 ml castor sugar
5 ml vanilla essence

15 ml cornflour
60 g flaked almonds
250 ml cream
250 g strawberries or fruit of choice, finely chopped

1 Preheat the oven to 160 °C.
2 Line a large swiss roll tin with a cooking bag or baking paper and spray with a non-stick spray.
3 Whisk the egg whites and vinegar until soft peaks form, then gradually beat in the castor sugar. The mixture should be thick and glossy. Add the vanilla and cornflour, and mix. Spread the mixture into the prepared tin and sprinkle with the almonds.
4 Bake for 20–25 minutes until firm. Turn out onto a sheet of greaseproof paper. Peel off the cooking bag or baking paper from the base and trim off the hard edges with scissors.
5 Leave to cool. Whip the cream until stiff. Spread onto the cooled meringue and top with the fruit.
6 Roll up like a swiss roll and place on a serving plate. Serve immediately or refrigerate for no more than 2–3 hours before serving.

*Rolled Pavlova*

*Lemon Meringue Ice Cream*

# Lemon Meringue Ice Cream
Serves 6–8

200 g ginger biscuits, crushed

100 g butter, melted

500 ml cream

250 ml Greek yoghurt

1 x 325 g jar lemon curd

grated rind and juice of 1–2 lemons

10 small meringues, broken into pieces

1 Line a 28 x 12 cm loaf tin with clingfilm. Mix the biscuits and butter. Sprinkle one third of the biscuit mixture over the base.
2 Pour the cream into a large mixing bowl and beat with an electric beater until stiff. Beat in the yoghurt. Gently fold in the lemon curd, rind and lemon juice, and lastly the meringues. Spoon half the cream mixture on top of the biscuit mixture in the loaf tin, sprinkle with a layer of crumbs and top with the remaining cream mixture.
3 Add a final layer of crumbs. Place into the freezer until firm.
4 Remove from the loaf tin, remove the clingfilm and serve sliced.


# Butterscotch Roulade
Serves 6

150 g dates, seeded and finely chopped

180 ml boiling water

5 ml bicarbonate of soda

60 g butter

160 ml brown sugar

2 extra-large eggs

180 ml self-raising flour

50 g pecan nuts, finely chopped

250 ml cream, whipped

SAUCE

125 ml brown sugar

180 ml cream

100 g butter

5 ml vanilla essence

1 Grease and line a 25 x 30 cm swiss roll tin with baking paper.
2 Combine the dates, boiling water and bicarbonate of soda in the bowl of a food processor. Leave to stand for 5 minutes to soften.
3 Add the butter and brown sugar, then process until smooth. Add the eggs and flour, and process further for a few minutes until the mixture is well combined, then mix in the nuts. Spoon the mixture into the prepared tin.
4 Bake at 180 °C for 15–20 minutes until firm to the touch. Remove from the oven and turn out onto a piece of greaseproof paper sprinkled with sugar. Peel away the baking paper, then leave to cool.
5 To prepare the sauce, combine all the ingredients and bring to the boil. Remove and cool.
6 Mix 80 ml of the cooled sauce into the whipped cream. Spread this over the cooled cake and gently roll it up using the sugared paper. Place on a serving dish, cut into slices and serve with the remaining sauce on the side.

# Pannacotta with Balsamic Strawberries

Serves 4

7.5 ml gelatine
60 ml water
250 ml cream
125 ml castor sugar
1 vanilla pod, split and scraped
250 ml thick Greek yoghurt

**BALSAMIC STRAWBERRIES**
250 g strawberries, sliced
30 ml balsamic vinegar
15–20 ml sugar

1 Sprinkle the gelatine over the water and set aside.
2 Combine the cream and castor sugar in a small saucepan and heat until almost boiling. Add the vanilla seeds and set aside for 30 minutes to infuse.
3 Dissolve the gelatine over hot water or in the microwave for 10 seconds on high. Add to the cream mixture.
4 Cool the mixture, then fold in the yoghurt. Spoon into four individual moulds that have been sprayed with non-stick cooking spray and refrigerate until set. Unmould and serve with the strawberries.
5 To prepare the strawberries: Place all the ingredients into a small saucepan and heat gently until the strawberries are slightly softened. Adjust the sugar to taste.


# Baked Lime Cheesecake

Serves 8–10

200 g chocolate digestive biscuits, crushed
80 g butter, softened
750 g thick cream cheese
250 ml castor sugar
4 whole eggs
2 egg yolks
juice of 4 limes or 2 lemons (±90 ml)

**TOPPING**
50 g chocolate
45 ml cream

1 Mix together the biscuits and butter to make a crumb crust. Press into the base of a 22 cm loose-bottomed cake tin that has been lined on the outside with a double layer of foil to prevent water from seeping in. Place in the fridge to set.
2 Beat the cream cheese gently until smooth, then add the castor sugar. Gently beat in the eggs and egg yolks. Finally add the lime or lemon juice.
3 Pour the mixture onto the chilled biscuit base. Place the cake tin in a roasting tray and pour hot water around the foil-wrapped cheesecake to come about halfway up the sides of the tin.
4 Bake in the oven at 180 °C for 50–60 minutes. The cheesecake should be set but will still have a slight wobble to it.
5 Leave it to cool slightly before removing the outer foil covering. When completely cool, place in the fridge to chill for about 1 hour before serving.
6 To make the topping, melt the chocolate and cream together, mix until smooth and drizzle over the cooled cheesecake.

*Pannacotta with Balsamic Strawberries*

*Chocolate Crème Brûlée*

# Black Forest Trifle

Serves 8

1 chocolate swiss roll

1 can pitted black cherries

15 ml custard powder mixed with 25 ml water

50 ml cherry liqueur

250 g thick cream cheese

1 x 397 g can condensed milk

125 ml lemon juice

250 ml cream

100 g chocolate, grated, for decoration

fresh cherries for decoration (optional)

1  Slice the swiss roll and line a serving dish with the slices (it can be either a glass bowl or a rectangular dish).
2  Drain the cherries and heat the juice in a small saucepan. Add the custard powder mixture and bring to the boil. Remove, then add the liqueur.
3  Sprinkle the cherries over the swiss roll base and pour over the juice mixture. Leave to cool.
4  Combine the cream cheese, condensed milk and lemon juice, and mix well. Pour this over the cherries and leave to set.
5  Whip the cream and spoon it over the cream cheese mixture. Cover with grated chocolate and decorate with fresh cherries, if available.

# Chocolate Crème Brûlée

Serves 6

500 ml cream

200 g good-quality dark chocolate, chopped

4 egg yolks

100 ml castor sugar plus extra for topping

1  Heat the cream in a saucepan until just boiling. Remove from the heat, add the chopped chocolate and mix until smooth.
2  Beat the egg yolks and castor sugar until pale, pour onto the hot chocolate mixture and mix until smooth. Spoon the mixture into 6 ramekins.
3  Place a tea towel in the base of a roasting tin and place the ramekins onto this. Pour water into the pan until it comes about halfway up the sides of the ramekins. Bake in the oven at 180 °C for 10–15 minutes until a skin forms and they are slightly set. Do not overcook.
4  Remove from the oven and chill for a few hours. Sprinkle the tops with castor sugar and melt with a blowtorch or under the grill until a sugar crust forms on top.
5  Serve immediately. Once the sugar has been placed on top, the dessert won't keep very long, as the hard caramel topping will soften on standing.

# Brown Bread Ice Cream Pudding
Serves 8

25 g mixed dried fruit
50 g glacé cherries (a mixture of red, green and
    yellow, if possible, quartered)
100 ml brandy
500 ml cream

100 ml castor sugar
250 ml grated fresh brown breadcrumbs
5 ml ground cinnamon
100 ml brown sugar

1  Combine the dried fruit and cherries in a bowl. Sprinkle with brandy, cover, and leave overnight.
2  Beat the cream and castor sugar until thickened. Chill in the freezer until almost set, stirring every half hour.
3  Meanwhile, combine the breadcrumbs, cinnamon and brown sugar and place on a baking tray. Toast at 200 °C for 5–10 minutes, until golden and caramelised. Leave to cool, then break up into small pieces.
4  Stir the soaked fruit and the caramelised breadcrumbs into the cream mix. Pour the mixture into a 1 litre pudding basin lined with clingfilm.
5  Freeze until solid. Remove 15 minutes before serving and unmould carefully.


# Gateau Diane
Serves 6

4 extra-large egg whites
250 ml castor sugar

**FILLING**
300 g plain dark chocolate
750 ml fresh cream
Flake® for decoration

1  Beat the egg whites until stiff, then add the castor sugar a little bit at a time, beating well after each addition.
2  Spread the mixture into 3 x 23 cm rounds on greaseproof paper. Bake at 140 °C for 50–60 minutes or longer until dry and crisp.
3  Break the chocolate into pieces, place in a glass bowl and microwave on medium for 2 minutes, stirring until melted. Whip the cream until it begins to thicken, then add the chocolate and continue beating until thick. Spread each meringue layer with the chocolate mixture, then stack the three layers on top of one another. Cover the sides and top completely. This must be done at least 3 hours before serving, but is better if done the day before, then refrigerated.
4  Decorate with the Flake®.

*Brown Bread Ice Cream Pudding*

*Roasted Fruit Salad with Brown Sugar Syrup*

# Roasted Fruit Salad with Brown Sugar Syrup

Serves 4–6

**BROWN SUGAR SYRUP**

100 ml water

30 ml lemon juice

125 g brown sugar

1 vanilla pod, split

**ROASTED FRUIT**

6 fresh figs, halved

2 nectarines, stoned and cut into wedges

6 plums, halved and stoned

300 g red grapes

50 g butter

50 ml castor sugar

1  To prepare the syrup, combine the water, lemon juice and brown sugar in a small saucepan. Scrape the seeds from the vanilla pod into the syrup mixture and bring to a gentle simmer, stirring until the sugar has dissolved. Boil for 5 minutes until slightly reduced and thickened. Remove and cool.
2  Preheat the oven to 200 °C.
3  Place the fruit in a single layer in a roasting dish. Dot with small pieces of butter and sprinkle with the castor sugar. Roast in the oven for 15 minutes. The fruits should still retain their shape but be soft.
4  Serve warm with the cooled syrup and a dollop of mascarpone cheese or ice cream. If specified fruit is unavailable, use any other soft seasonal fruit.

# That Impossibly Easy Coconut Pudding

*Why impossible? Because it is impossibly easy to make!*

Serves 4–6

4 eggs

125 g softened butter, cut into small cubes

125 ml cake flour

125 ml milk

250 ml sugar

250 ml desiccated coconut

1 x 400 g can coconut milk

1  Preheat the oven to 180 °C.
2  Grease a 23 cm square ovenproof dish.
3  Place all the ingredients in a food processor and blend well. Pour into the prepared dish and bake for 1 hour.
4  Cool to room temperature before cutting into serving portions. Serve with cream or ice cream.

# Bar One® Cheesecake

Serves 8–10

200 g packet chocolate digestive biscuits, crushed
80 g butter, softened
60 ml water
15 ml gelatine
500 g thick cream cheese, softened

5 ml vanilla essence
125 ml castor sugar
3 x Bar One®, finely chopped
250 ml cream, whipped

1   Combine the biscuits and butter and press evenly into the base of a 20 cm springform tin. Refrigerate until firm.
2   Pour the water into a small heatproof bowl and sprinkle in the gelatine. Microwave on high for 10 seconds or stand in a pan of simmering water until dissolved. Cool slightly.
3   Beat the cream cheese, vanilla essence and castor sugar with an electric beater until smooth. Beat in the gelatine, then stir in the Bar One® pieces. Fold in the cream.
4   Spoon the mixture into the prepared tin and refrigerate until set.

# Orange and Almond Cake

*A delicious almost cheesecake-type cake made without any flour*
Serves 8–10

2 large oranges
250 ml castor sugar
200 g ground almonds
2.5 ml baking powder

6 eggs
45 ml lemon juice
icing sugar

1   Place the whole oranges into a pan and cover with water. Bring to the boil, reduce the heat, cover and simmer for 2 hours or until the oranges are tender, topping up with water as needed. Remove from the water and leave to cool.
2   Preheat the oven to 180 °C and grease a 23 cm tin. Cut the oranges into chunks and remove the pips. Do not peel the oranges.
3   Place the orange chunks in a food processor and process together with the remaining ingredients until well mixed.
4   Transfer to the prepared tin and bake for 45–60 minutes until well risen and firm to the touch. Cool, then dust with icing sugar.

*Orange and Almond Cake*

*Creamy Strawberry Dessert*

# Mango Ice Cream
Serves 4

3 medium-sized mangoes, peeled
juice of 1 lemon
250 ml sugar

2 extra-large eggs
250 ml cream

1 Cut the mango flesh from the mangoes and discard the stones. Purée the fruit in a food processor or blender, then add the lemon juice. Add 185 ml of the sugar and blend until smooth. Pour into a bowl, cover with clingfilm and refrigerate.
2 Separate the eggs and beat the yolks until thick and creamy. Beat the egg whites until stiff peaks form.
3 Whip the cream until it just starts to thicken, then gradually add the remaining sugar and beat until soft peaks form.
4 Fold in the egg yolks and whipped whites. Gently fold into the mango purée. Pour into a mould and freeze. For a smoother ice cream, beat again when it is just starting to form ice crystals, then re-freeze.

# Creamy Strawberry Dessert
Serves 10

1 x 397 g can condensed milk
100 ml fresh lemon juice
250 g strawberries, cleaned and hulled
250 g smooth cream cheese
5 ml vanilla

15 ml gelatine
45 ml water
250 ml cream, whipped
extra cream and strawberries for decoration

1 Combine the condensed milk and lemon juice in a food processor, and process until well blended. Add the strawberries and process until smooth. Add the cream cheese and vanilla and mix.
2 Sprinkle the gelatine over the water and leave to form a soft sponge, then soften the gelatine over hot water or in the microwave on high for 10 seconds.
3 With the machine running, add the gelatine to the strawberry mixture and mix well.
4 Gently fold in the whipped cream and pour into a serving dish. Place in the fridge to set.
5 Decorate with the extra cream and strawberries before serving.

# Marinades & Rubs

# Fresh Herb Rub

60 ml chopped fresh thyme
60 ml chopped fresh rosemary
60 ml chopped fresh origanum
250 ml chopped fresh parsley

5 ml crushed garlic
10 ml sea salt
5 ml freshly ground black pepper
125 ml olive oil

1 Place all the ingredients except the olive oil into the bowl of a food processor. With the motor running, gradually pour in the oil until the mixture is well blended.
2 Rub into steak, cover and rest in the fridge before cooking.

# Mustard Rub

60 ml chopped fresh parsley
15 ml whole grain mustard
5 ml freshly ground black pepper

10 ml crushed garlic
5 ml salt

Combine all the ingredients and rub onto steak or patties. Rest in the fridge for at least 30 minutes before cooking.

# Store Cupboard Rub

45 ml sugar
15 ml paprika
5 ml garlic powder
2 ml chilli powder

10 ml lemon pepper
15 ml dried sage
5 ml dried basil
5 ml dried rosemary

1 Combine all the ingredients.
2 Brush the selected meat with a little olive oil, then rub in the mixture.

# Beer Marinade

5 ml Tabasco® Sauce
45 ml cider vinegar
340 ml beer
25 ml whole grain mustard

60 ml soy sauce
10 ml crushed garlic
1 small onion, finely chopped
freshly ground black pepper

1 Combine all the ingredients in a small bowl.
2 Pour over steak and refrigerate for at least 3 hours or overnight.

# Tamarind and Orange Marinade

*Great for chicken, lamb, seafood or duck*

grated rind of 1 orange

80 ml orange juice

60 ml honey

80 ml tamarind paste

80 ml soy sauce

1   Combine all the ingredients and mix well.
2   Slash the chicken portions a few times, place into a plastic bag or suitable container and pour over the marinade. Seal well, then refrigerate for a few hours or, preferably, overnight.
3   Remove the chicken from the marinade and cook over a medium heat until done, basting frequently with the marinade.

NOTE: Tamarind paste is available from oriental shops. It can also be made by soaking about 25 ml tamarind pulp in 100 ml warm water, then pressing it through a sieve and discarding the pulp and seeds and using only the remaining liquid.

# Jerk Marinade

*The word 'jerk' refers to a seasoning blend that is used in Jamaica and the Caribbean. Most Jamaican food lovers agree that there are three ingredients that jerk seasoning mixes must have in order to taste authentic – allspice, scotch bonnet chillies and thyme. The remaining ingredients may vary. If you are apprehensive about using the very hot chillies, then replace them with a milder one. This is suitable for chicken, lamb, pork or beef.*

5 ml ground allspice

5 ml ground cinnamon

5 ml dried thyme

1.5 ml ground nutmeg

15 ml soft brown sugar

2 cloves garlic, crushed

1 bunch spring onions, white parts only, finely chopped

15 ml white wine vinegar

45 ml olive oil

15 ml lime juice

1 scotch bonnet chilli, finely chopped

1   Combine all the ingredients to form a thick paste. Rub this mixture well into the meat portions. Place into a plastic bag or suitable container and leave for a few hours or overnight.
2   Cook over a medium fire until cooked through.

NOTE: True Jamaican jerk must be barbecued. The traditional way is to slow roast the meat at a low temperature over a fire fuelled by allspice branches that give the meat a sweet, smoky, spicy flavour. As we do not have access to allspice branches in South Africa, use hard wood to make your fire or add a few smoking chips to your barbecue.

# Lavender and Honey Marinade

*This has a wonderfully subtle flavour with the aroma of lavender. Adding a few lavender twigs to the fire will enhance the lavender flavour. Suitable for chicken portions, or pork fillet or chops.*

small bunch of lavender flowers
grated rind of 1 orange
60 ml orange juice
2 cloves garlic, crushed

25 ml honey
30 ml olive oil
10 ml fresh thyme, chopped

1   Strip off the lavender flowers and chop them roughly. Combine with the remaining ingredients and mix well.
2   If using chicken, slash the flesh. Rub the marinade into the chicken or pork. Place in a plastic bag, seal well and refrigerate overnight.
3   Remove the meat from the marinade and cook on a barbecue over a medium heat until cooked, basting with any remaining marinade during the cooking time.


# Mint and Yoghurt Marinade

*A lovely light marinade with a wonderful minty flavour*

125 ml plain yoghurt
15 ml honey
50 ml lemon juice

30 ml olive oil
60 ml fresh mint, chopped
salt and freshly ground black pepper

Combine the ingredients and mix well. Use to marinate poultry or game.


# Rosemary and Chilli Marinade

*Suitable for chicken, lamb or pork*

120 ml olive oil
grated rind of 1 lemon
60 ml lemon juice
1 large red chilli, finely chopped

10 ml chopped garlic
25 ml chopped fresh rosemary leaves
salt and freshly ground black pepper

1   Mix all the ingredients for the marinade and pour it over the meat in a plastic bag. Seal the bag well and place it in the fridge overnight.
2   Remove the meat from the marinade and cook over a medium heat on the barbecue until done, basting with marinade during cooking.

# White Wine Marinade

*Best for fish, chicken and pork*

175 ml white wine

grated rind and juice of 1 lemon

45 ml olive oil

2 cloves garlic, crushed

3 spring onions, finely chopped

1 bay leaf

pinch of salt

Mix all the ingredients together and pour over the meat or fish. Cover and place in the fridge, turning a couple of times.

# Spicy Yoghurt Marinade

*Great for fish and chicken, particularly chicken breasts*

250 ml plain yoghurt or buttermilk

juice of 1 lemon

2.5 ml turmeric

2.5 ml ground paprika

2.5 ml ground ginger

pinch of dried chilli flakes

2 cloves garlic, crushed

handful fresh coriander, finely chopped

salt and white pepper

Combine all the ingredients and mix well. Use to coat the meat before cooking.

# Red Wine Marinade

*Good for meat and game*

500 ml red wine

30 ml brown sugar

1 onion, sliced

1 carrot, peeled and sliced

1 stick celery, sliced

handful of fresh thyme

1 clove garlic, crushed

1 bay leaf

1 large strip orange peel

3 whole cloves

coarse salt

Combine all the ingredients in small pan over very low heat and simmer gently for 10 minutes. Cool completely. Marinate the meat for 12–24 hours, covered in the fridge, turning a couple of times.

# Index

*Page numbers in **bold** represent photographs*

## Metric Measures

| | | | | | |
|---|---|---|---|---|---|
| 1 litre | = | 4 cups | 45 ml | = | 3 tablespoons |
| 750 ml | = | 3 cups | 30 ml | = | 2 tablespoons |
| 500 ml | = | 2 cups | 15 ml | = | 1 tablespoon |
| 325 ml | = | 1½ cups | 20 ml | = | 4 teaspoons |
| 250 ml | = | 1 cup | 10 ml | = | 2 teaspoons |
| 200 ml | = | ¾ cup | 8 ml | = | 1½ teaspoon |
| 125 ml | = | ½ cup | 5 ml | = | 1 teaspoon |
| 80 ml | = | ⅓ cup | 3 ml | = | ½ teaspoon |
| 60 ml | = | ¼ cup/4 tablespoons | 2 ml | = | ¼ teaspoon |